Home Office Research Study 201

'Tell Them So They Listen':
Messages from Young People in Custody

by
Juliet Lyon, Catherine Dennison & Anita Wilson
Trust for the Study of Adolescence

**A Research, Development and
Statistics Directorate Report**

London: Home Office

Home Office Research Studies

The Home Office Research Studies are reports on research undertaken by or on behalf of the Home Office. They cover the range of subjects for which the Home Secretary has responsibility. Titles in the series are listed at the back of this report (copies are available from the address on the back cover). Other publications produced by the Research, Development and Statistics Directorate include Research Findings, the Research Bulletin, Statistical Bulletins and Statistical Papers.

The Research, Development and Statistics Directorate

 RDS is part of the Home Office. The Home Office's purpose is to build a safe, just and tolerant society in which the rights and responsibilities of individuals, families and communities are properly balanced and the protection and security of the public are maintained.

RDS is also a part of the Government Statistical Service (GSS). One of the GSS aims is to inform Parliament and the citizen about the state of the nation and provide a window on the work and performance of government, allowing the impact of government policies and actions to be assessed.

Therefore -

Research Development and Statistics Directorate exists to improve policy making, decision taking and practice in support of the Home Office purpose and aims, to provide the public and Parliament with information necessary for informed debate and to publish information for future use.

"The views expressed in this report are those of the authors, not necessarily those of the Home Office (nor do they reflect Government policy)."

First published 2000

Application for reproduction should be made to the Information and Publications Group, Room 201, Home Office, 50 Queen Anne's Gate, London SW1H 9AT.

©Crown copyright 2000 ISBN 1 84082 437 9
ISSN 0072 6435

Foreword

Rt. Hon. Paul Boateng M.P.

I am very pleased to have been asked to provide the foreword to this important report, which was commissioned by George Howarth, MP during his period as Parliamentary Under Secretary at the Home Office.

Too often in the past, policies aimed at helping young people on the margins of society have been drawn up without consulting a most important group – the young people themselves. That is why we decided that we wanted to hear from the young people at the sharp end of the youth justice system, to hear their views on how the criminal justice system has treated them, to hear their opinions of current initiatives, and most importantly, their hopes and aspirations for the future.

This report does not always make for comfortable reading. But as the title of the report tells us, it is important that we listen to what the young people have to say. It is heartening to read that the young people themselves want decent lives and decent futures for themselves and their children. We share that aspiration with them.

Listening to what these young people have to say should help us in the ambitious programme of work we have undertaken to reform the youth justice system - and reduce re-offending. The most important gift we can make to the young is to use the lessons we have learnt, not least from this work, to act decisively to secure a better future.

Acknowledgments

The Authors would like to thank all the young people who participated.

We are grateful to the governors and staff in the ten young offender establishments, who enabled us to carry out the focus groups with them.

We would like to acknowledge the advice and support of the Research Development and Statistics Directorate and the Young Offender Group in helping us carry out this research.

Lastly, we should like to thank our colleagues at TSA for their support, in particular Helen Richardson who took on the difficult task of transcribing the focus group recordings and Dr John Coleman for his involvement in the project.

Contents

Executive Summary

'Tell Them So They Listen'
Messages from Young People in Custody

Tackling youth crime, reducing social exclusion and reforming youth justice are key targets for the Government. There is a new emphasis on seeing young people as part of the solution, not just as part of the problem.

Home Office Ministers requested that focus group research should be conducted so that they could hear directly from children and young people in custody. Ministers believed that this information could usefully inform the direction of policy and practice.

The Home Office Research Develpment and Statistics Directorate together with the Young Offender Group commissioned the Trust for the Study of Adolescence (TSA) to undertake this research.

The findings and the key messages from young people offer a powerful reinforcement of the Government's agenda for crime reduction. They point to the potential for the increased involvement of marginalised young people not only in consultation about, but in the process of, effecting change.

The Focus Groups

Focus groups took place in ten prisons (7 male and 3 female) that hold young offenders. These establishments were chosen for their regional spread, ethnically diverse populations and wide range of offence categories. Three of the groups (2 of young men and 1 of young women) were restricted to those under the age of eighteen. Participants were selected on a random basis from the sentenced young offender population and invited to attend. All were volunteers.

Eighty four young people (58 young men and 26 young women) took part in the ten groups. Nineteen young people were black, Asian or mixed race.

Discussion focused on three main areas:

- Life before and leading up to entering prison
- Experiences of custody
- Hopes, fears and plans for the future.

Within these areas it was intended that young people would explore their experience of, and views on: parenting; local authority care; education; employment; housing; drug and alcohol use; violence and bullying; and the criminal justice system.

Almost all the young people worked hard during the session to put across their ideas and concerns clearly. They maintained a high degree of concentration and listened with respect to one another.

From the discussions, insights emerged with clear implications for policy and practice. The picture the young men and women presented was complex. They could see no single or easy solutions. In their view immediate change is called for on a number of levels. They wanted to break into what they saw as "the same circle, over and over again".

The Background to Offending

In reviewing their pathways into crime, the young people placed considerable emphasis on self-determination, choice and responsibility. Most believed that they had had a choice not to offend. They had nearly all received warnings from adults about getting into trouble.

> *But it goes in one ear and out the other innit? That's when you're young and don't give a fuck!*   *(Young man)*

Many believed that their parents, particularly their mothers, had tried their best to intervene:

> *She tried everything, tried everything and it's not worked has it? It's down to me at the end of the day. I know what's got to be done. They tear their hair out trying to help don't they? They try everything but at the end of the day it's down to you.*   *(Young man)*

From discussion in the groups, a more complex picture developed. While most young people still held to the view that it was 'down to them', it was clear that many had had to struggle to survive in difficult and disrupted circumstances. They talked about "rough, nasty areas" where violence, crime, drug use, unemployment and poverty were just part of everyday life. A number felt seriously let down by adults who could have cared for them or helped them.

Some young people saw their route into crime as almost inevitable:

> *We've all been through social services, foster, children's homes, getting kicked out of school, secure unit.... I'm sure we've all been through that road. It's like a journey and we've all collected our tickets along the way.* (*Young woman*)

For some, particularly those using hard drugs, involvement in crime had become a way of life.

> *When you're a smackhead, it's the same thing, you go out, you rob, you graft, you sell your stuff, you score, you're mongy when you get up, you do the same every single day. Nothing occurs in your head, nothing just that.* (*Young woman*)

The majority felt that once they had become involved in the cycle of offending it was very hard to get out. Their view that it was better never to get involved in the first place supports the Government's emphasis on early intervention and prevention. The key messages from young people about change in the community were these:

- To prevent children and young people becoming involved in crime, design interventions to target the very young.
- Don't blame parents, focus on improving communication between parents and teenagers.
- Clean up the estates and improve poor living conditions, where violence, drug dealing and crime are just part of everyday life.
- Marginalised young people, including those who don't or can't go to school, still want to learn and should be involved in education.
- Disrupted lives can be a route to offending, children and young people in local authority care need continuity and stability, someone, or just a few people they can trust and rely on over time.
- Young people are influenced a great deal by their friends, so find ways to make positive uses of peer group pressure.
- To prevent offending, tackle drug and alcohol abuse, in particular, target hard drug dealers and suppliers and take drugs off the streets and out of schools and colleges.

Within the Criminal Justice System

Young people were very critical of unprofessional adults and unprofessional services in the criminal justice system. They talked about a 'sloppiness' in the delivery of services which was both frustrating and easy to exploit.

They described being 'processed' through a system which was often hard to understand or unfair. High staff turnover and ineffective practice meant there was no one you could refer to or trust.

What can they do for you? They can't do nowt for you, they just sit there and take notes. They don't do nothing for you.(Young man)

Above all, young people wanted to be treated with respect and to be taken seriously by professional adults. Many gave detailed practical examples of disrespectful treatment, clear abuse of power by adults in authority and, in some cases, incidents involving overt racism or violence. This has important implications for the selection, training and management of staff who work with vulnerable and volatile children and young people.

These were the young people's messages about change in the criminal justice system. Many of their concerns are reflected in the Youth Justice Board's widespread programme of reform.

- Tackle racism in every area of the criminal justice system and ensure fair, respectful and appropriate treatment for young black people.
- Pay particular attention to improving relations between the police and young people.
- Court processes should be quicker and clearer. Judges and magistrates should be more in touch with young people's lives.
- Sentencing should be fairer, eradicating any gender, race and regional bias. Community sentences must have more credibility and relevance.
- Youth justice and probation workers should be visible, consistent and effective.

Being in Prison

Many young people spoke of being scared, humiliated and de-personalised on reaching prison.

You just feel like a catalogue delivery, like you're nothing. 'Here's your delivery', that's it and you're just given a number...
(Young woman)

A few spoke of 'safe' or 'straightforward' staff, but the majority criticised the way staff treated them.

...they come here and suddenly they're working with a load of kids that they can shout at and they talk down to you. (Young man)

Many of the young people said that they wanted to use their time in custody constructively. They were frustrated by what they saw as petty rules and procedures; poor induction or sentence planning; and the difficulty of completing education, cognitive skills and parenthood courses which they valued.

The majority saw prison as a dislocating experience, unconnected to their lives outside. They were very critical of the lack of preparation for life back in the community.

Like you get one town visit and then you're out, bam, you're on the road and you've been outside of society for years and then, bam, you're back. It's like, even in your own town, you're in a time warp. Everything's changed. (Young man)

The programme to improve regime quality and standards embodied in the new Prison Service Order aims to create a more structured and caring environment for under 18 year olds. The young people made these points about what needs to change in prison:

- Staff should treat children and young people with respect. They should be trained to understand that young people are growing up while they are in prison.
- Make prisons safe for young people by tackling bullying, racism and offending behaviour in the institution.
- Prison rules and procedures should be clear and fair if they are to be understood by young people.
- Make proper use of induction, sentence planning and personal officer schemes to guide young people through their time in prison.
- To reduce the risk of re-offending, offending behaviour programmes, education, and preparation for work must all be given priority.
- Tackle the use of illegal drugs in prison.
- Reduce the use of prescribed drugs by improving health care and emotional support for young people.
- Prisons for young people should be much more connected to the outside world: families, carers, friends, youth justice workers.
- Prepare young people properly for release and create opportunities to adjust more gradually to life in the community.

Preparation and Planning for Life Outside

Young people gave the impression that they had used a considerable amount of time in prison to think about their hopes, fears and prospects for life outside. They often talked aspirationally about their future lives. At the same time they were critically aware of the difficulties of going back to what they described as 'a shit life out there' and of the high probability of their re-offending.

> *I'm getting out in 12 weeks, and I'm getting so scared, because it's easy to say 'I'm not going to get into trouble', but it really creeps on me, like trouble just finds me.*   *(Young woman)*

Drug users believed that they were particularly at risk of re-offending.

> *They just think you can come to jail, stop your drugs, go out and you're alright, but it doesn't work like that. It's temptation, not withdrawal, it's temptation nowt else.*   *(Young woman)*

The pressing need for support and someone to talk to after prison was stated, or implied, by most of the young people. Many believed that decent housing, continuing education, real jobs and having enough money to live on would help them to survive in the community.

Being a parent was seen as a primary reason to stop offending. The young parents in the groups believed that they had a responsibility to stop their own children getting into trouble.

> *I'm going to say 'look at me, this is what I've done, this is the mistakes I've made. What do you want to do in life? Do you want to turn out like me or do you want to sort your life out and that?'*
>   *(Young woman)*

The young people's views on the factors which led to their initial involvement with crime and now to the high probability of their re-offending would endorse the Government's programme to target social inequalities as a way of tackling youth crime. Their need for continuing support after prison should be met in part by the introduction of the Detention and Training Order. After-care for those over the age of eighteen may not yet have been addressed fully.

These were the young people's key messages about life after prison:

- To reduce the risk of re-offending, young people need after-care and close support following their release from prison.

- Young people need particular help to stay off drugs, preferably from ex-users who know from experience how difficult this process is.
- Provide young people with practical help with housing and resettlement and create drug free hostels.
- 16 to 18 year olds leaving prison need adequate benefits or wages to survive in the community.
- Help young people to prepare for, and to get real jobs, possibly by setting up agencies for young ex-offenders.
- Young parents in prison want to be good parents to their own children. They may need support to overcome difficulties in trying to resume their responsibilities.
- Marginalised young people need specific opportunities to be listened to and become involved in their communities.

Discussion of the Findings

Four main themes emerged from the focus groups. The first was personal responsibility. While many of their ideas for change require action by others, young people believe that principally it is up to them to change their lives.

This points to the possibility that offending behaviour might be reduced by increasing opportunities for youth participation and involvement both in the community and in secure settings. Young people want to be included.

Secondly, young people talked a lot about their families. Some spoke of close support but many referred to disrupted lives, absent fathers, premature deaths and changing family relationships. Most said that they wanted to parent their own children differently. Whether their experiences had been positive or negative, it was clear that the young people thought parenting and the role of the family were important. Support and guidance, both for parents of teenagers, and for young parents themselves, is called for.

Thirdly, young people in custody have had considerable contact with professional adults and services. In the main, these contacts have proved unsatisfactory. Their views endorse radical reform of the youth justice system.

Lastly, the young people stated that they wanted decent lives and decent futures for themselves and their children. Decent lives did not involve crime or drugs. Crime reduction was very much on their agenda too. They hoped that their voices would be heard, and their ideas for change taken seriously.

As one young person said:

'Tell them so they listen'.

1 Introduction

Tackling youth crime, reducing social exclusion and reforming youth justice are key targets for the Government. There is a new emphasis on seeing young people as part of the solution, not just as part of the problem[1]. Home Office Ministers requested that focus group research should be conducted so that they could hear directly from children and young people in custody. Ministers wanted young people's views on their lives before custody; their experiences of the criminal justice system; their time in custody; and their hopes and plans for after release. Ministers believed that this information could usefully inform the direction of policy and practice.

The Home Office Research Development and Statistics Directorate together with the Young Offender Group commissioned the Trust for the Study of Adolescence (TSA) to undertake this research.

TSA[2] has an established commitment to:

- applying research to practice to improve the quality and standards of work with young people in the youth justice system
- listening to young people and including them in the research process.

George Howarth, at that time Parliamentary Under Secretary of State at the Home Office, launched the focus group research project in November 1998 at the Young Offender Governor's Conference. He stated that:

While there is much we can learn from the research literature on best practice and what works, I believe we can learn a lot more if we listen to the young people involved themselves... I believe that when we and colleagues in other departments shape and plan provision we should have in our minds what the young people themselves feel is important.

TSA first submitted this report of the research findings to the Home Office in July 1999.

---

1   Keynote speech by the Rt. Hon. Paul Boateng, Minister of State at the Home Office, at the 'In From The Margins' Conference, November 1998.
2   See note on TSA and the Authors.

The Context

As of the 31st December 1999 there were 10,505 young people aged between 15 and 21 years in Prison Service custody in England and Wales. The vast majority, 10,058, were young men and 2,085 of these were aged between 15 and 17. There were 447 young women in custody, 83 were aged between 15 and 17. Eighty one per cent of the young offender population were white; 14 per cent black; 3 per cent South Asian; and 2 per cent Chinese or from 'other' ethnic groups. The most common offence for all young people in custody is burglary. Rates for reconviction within 2 years vary from 40 per cent, for those who have no previous convictions prior to entering custody, to 95 per cent for young men with 11 or more convictions[3].

Young people in custody have been shown to be a particularly marginalised group. The Chief Inspector of Prisons in his report 'Young Prisoners: A Thematic Review' (1997) states that a substantial proportion have had contact with social services or have spent time being 'looked after'. Most have been failed by the education system. Over half of his sample had been excluded from school. The majority were unemployed before entering custody; and most had been involved with drug or alcohol misuse at some time.

Many young prisoners struggle to maintain family links and a significant proportion of both male and female young offenders report that they are already parents themselves. The Chief Inspector's report also showed that a high percentage of young people have suffered physical, sexual or emotional abuse prior to custody. Experience of loss and bereavement is common[4].

A number of young people are very vulnerable when they enter custody. The incidence of mental health problems amongst young offenders is significant both before and during their time in prison. Rates of suicide, and self-injurious behaviours are high amongst young prisoners[5].

Young men and women in custody are an especially volatile group and present many challenges to those who work with them. The numbers of assaults and adjudications for this age group are high compared with those for adults in prison.

Whilst a number of studies have looked at the routes that bring young offenders into custody and looked at the needs, and behaviour, of young offenders whilst they are there, little research has started from looking at the narratives of the young people themselves. The concerns they raise and experiences they describe are our starting point here.

---

3   Information and statistics provided by the Home Office Research and Statistics Directorate and the Young Offender group.
4   Boswell (1995) documents the high incidence of both abuse and loss in the lives of Section 53 offenders.
5   Liebling (1991); HM Chief Inspector of Prisons (1999).

Methods

Focus Groups were selected as the most appropriate methodology for this project. They enable the gathering of information from a group of people through group discussion. Because the members of the group are peers, and due to the fact that they talk to one another as much as to the facilitator, the discussion allows access to their shared beliefs and understandings. By creating opportunities for group members to question and explain things to each other, the focus group process allows insight into the construction of meanings between participants. In addition, it is thought that focus groups facilitate rather than inhibit openness. Focus groups are, it is argued, 'more than the sum of separate individual interviews'[6].

The disadvantages of this methodology in a prison setting are that some young people could find it difficult to talk about personal issues in a randomly selected group. Some might 'censor' their contributions to avoid repercussions later. In this context, peer influence may have acted to inhibit discussion about positive aspects of the criminal justice system. Facilitators needed to be mindful of these issues and work to mitigate them, without putting the young people under pressure.

Though the nature of focus group methodology means that participants take the discussion in directions they want to develop, a number of topics and suggested questions were identified in advance[7]. The proposed outline areas for discussion were forwarded to Ministers and advisors and revised to reflect their recommendations and interests prior to piloting. The schedule focused on three main areas:

- Life before and leading up to entering prison
- Experiences of custody
- Hopes, fears and plans for the future.

Within these areas it was intended that young people would explore their experience of, and views on, parenting; local authority care; education; employment; housing; drug and alcohol use; violence and bullying; and the criminal justice system. We wanted to know their views on what support they had received from adults both outside, and inside, the prison. What could have made a difference to their lives? What, and who, could have prevented them from becoming involved in offending? And what could stop them re-offending?

The outline areas for discussion were piloted in two establishments. No substantive changes were needed and the material from these groups is included within the main sample.

---

6   Morgan (1996, p.139).
7   Appendix I presents examples of the questions that were asked on each of these topics.

The Institutions

Focus groups took place in ten prisons that held young offenders. Seven of these were male and three were female establishments. They were Aylesbury; Bullwood Hall; Feltham; Huntercombe; Lancaster Farms; Moorland; New Hall; Styal; Swinfen Hall and Thorn Cross. These institutions were selected on the advice of the Research and Statistics Directorate and the Young Offender Group. They were chosen for their regional spread, ethnically diverse populations and wide range of offence categories. Three of the groups, one of young women and two of young men, were restricted to participants under eighteen.

Within each establishment the groups' participants were selected on a random basis from the sentenced young offender population. Remand prisoners were excluded from the study as we were advised that their time in custody is subject to different rules and conditions and that their experience of custody may, therefore, be different.

Individual members of staff within the prisons were asked by governors to co-ordinate the focus groups. To arrive at a random selection they extracted a list of prisoners within the target age group from the LIDS system, the prison's central database of prisoners, in order of ascending age. Names were selected from the list at regular intervals, dependent on the size of the population. Each individual selected was invited to attend by the person liaising with the research team. The young people were briefed about the nature and purpose of the groups. Where this invitation was declined the next person on the list was asked to participate, until the number for each group reached between eight and ten.

The Young People

Eighty four young people took part in the ten groups. Of these, twenty six were young women. Thirty were known to be under the under the age of eighteen because they participated in the three age restricted groups or declared their age in the course of one of the other groups. Based on our own visual categorisations, nineteen young people were black, Asian or mixed race. A further two young people described themselves as 'travellers'. There were no young people with a noticeable disability, although some referred to chronic health problems. All of the young people were convicted, though a small number were awaiting sentencing.

These young people have reached the end point of the criminal justice system. Most have experienced a range of interventions prior to entering prison from members of different professional groups including probation, education, social services, police and courts.

The Focus Groups

The ten focus groups took place between December 1998 and March 1999. Each group was facilitated by two members of the research team. This enabled us to monitor the direction of the discussion and to ensure that all topic areas were covered.

Groups were held in a wide variety of settings. These included visits areas, rooms in health care and education units, and a YMCA Youth Centre on a unit.

Information about the briefings given to the young people usually emerged at the start of the groups. Members of one group said that they had been told very little other than that there were "two doctors coming in to talk to us about our behaviour". This proved the exception and most groups had been well briefed and knew what to expect. Members of another group, for example, said that they expected the discussion to cover:

What goes on in prisons and what our views are.

What really happens.

How can we make it better, stop re-offending.

See if there are any needs in prison.

With one exception the groups took place with no officers or other prison staff present. In the exception, officers stayed within the large room, but were out of earshot of the discussion.

At the beginning of each group the facilitators confirmed where they were from and explained the aims of the session. The young people were assured that their contributions to the discussion would remain anonymous and to this end we did not take the names of the participants. After gaining the agreement of group participants, all the focus groups were tape recorded and later transcribed.

In order to start from a common experience we began each session by asking young people about their first impressions on coming into prison. This invariably prompted most people to join in the discussion.

Each group ran for approximately one and a half hours, including a ten minute break for refreshments. Almost all the young people worked extremely hard during the session to put across their ideas and concerns clearly. They maintained a high degree of concentration and listened with respect to one another.

Although many young people were surprised that Home Office Ministers should want to hear from them, most appreciated having the opportunity to express their views and to put their ideas across. A few thought that there might be no point in saying what they felt and believed and what they wanted to change. It was hard to put thoughts into words and anyway no one would listen and nothing would change.

> *It's hard to explain, you don't know if you're saying things right because you're only used to this sort of thing. But you're trying to say something and you're thinking, 'oh', you're used to people saying 'no, that's wrong'. But at the end of the day nothing's going to get done, this tape recordings not going to do nothing.*
>
> *(Young woman)*

For most of the young people, the discussions had proved positive in themselves. Having someone to talk to mattered.

> *I think it's good to talk in a group, me, with people who are not involved in the prison.* 			*(Under 18 young woman)*

Opportunities were given at the end of each focus group to re-state messages to Government. Following a preliminary analysis of the material, letters of thanks and an outline summary of the findings were returned to each of the establishments for distribution to the young people who participated.

The Report

The findings from the research are structured in three main sections corresponding to the chronology of events in the young people's lives. Part 2, 'The Background to Offending', details their perspectives on their lives before first entering custody. Part 3, 'Being in Prison', describes their views on their time in custody. Part 4, 'Preparation and Planning for Life Outside Prison' looks to their plans, fears and expectations following their release.

Throughout the report the findings are linked to relevent research evidence which often endorses what the young people discussed in the focus groups.

We have aimed to represent accurately what the young people have said to us. To this end we have presented their points in their own words as much as space allows. The use of text set out in boxes throughout the report allows for the introduction of extended dialogue from the groups on some key topics. We have not 'cleaned', censored or 'distilled' what was said.

The final part of this report to Ministers sets out the key messages we have drawn from what the young people said.

2 The Background to Offending

To find out more about the background to offending, we guided the discussion towards such topics as what it was like for the young people growing up in their family and/ or in care; how they had found education; their experiences of the courts and the police; whether they had had involvement with drugs or alcohol before entering custody; views on community service or other non-custodial programmes and whether they thought anyone could have stopped them from offending.

Young people gave some thoughtful and forthright answers. They talked about growing up in bad areas, with high levels of crime and drug use; being labelled by education as a 'problem' and subsequently being excluded; they gave explanations for beginning offending; and they were critical of the way they had been treated by the criminal justice system. Many thought that their families were not to blame for their involvement in crime.

Family: 'They do their best for you at the end of the day'

A central focus of each discussion was young people's experience of family life. Many young people fiercely defended their parents and the upbringing they had received. Few felt that the way they had been parented had influenced them to become involved with offending.

> *My mum's tried her best with me, there's officers in this jail who say it's your parents' fault that you're in jail, it's not, my mum tried her best with me.*   (Young woman)

Many were aware of theories attributing crime to family background[8] and rejected this notion.

> *There are a lot of people that say 'oh my parents didn't treat me right' that's bullshit man.*   (Under 18 young man)

A minority thought that they had been affected negatively by their parenting.

---

8   Characteristics of families (e.g. teenage parenting, large family size and parental divorce) and parenting styles (e.g. coercive/hostile parenting, poor supervision, abuse and neglect) have been consistently shown to be central factors associated with the development of delinquent lifestyles (see Farrington, 1996; Rutter, Giller and Hagell, 1998).

The way I am, the way I'm violent and that, it's because of my family and the way I've been brought up and that. All me uncles and me dad, even me mum's been to jail for violence and all that, I've got brothers and cousins who've all been to jail for violence, and I didn't grow up all cushy with a silver spoon up me arse or anything like that, I grew up the hard way.   *(Young man)*

Few young people had grown up in intact two-parent families[9]. In one group of young women there had been no mention of fathers until the facilitator remarked on this:

Q: I've just realised we've spent the whole time and nobody's talked about dads

A: That's because there's no dads to talk about!

A: We don't need dads, at the end of the day a child needs it's mum.   *(Young woman)*

Many young people had had only occasional contact with their father whilst growing up, due to parental divorce or relationship breakup, or due to their dad being in prison[10]. Some young people stated that several members of their family, including their father, had been involved with crime and had spent time in prison[11].

My dad's been in jail, me eldest brother's been in jail, me second eldest brother's been in jail, I've been in jail, me youngest brother's going the same way.   *(Young man)*

Often as a consequence of their father's absence many young people talked about having a great deal of respect for, and a strong attachment to their mother[12]. Mothers had stood by them and supported them throughout, for example:

A: Me mum's right, she's been there all the time me mum, but not me dad

Q: Did your mum worry that you might end up inside?

A: Yeah, she knew me mum. Because I were on smack, she knew I were going to get locked up because she knew I was having it and everything. She never kicked me out of the house, she just stood by me all the way through it.   *(Young man)*

---

9   Graham and Bowling (1995) found that growing up in one-parent families increased the likelihood that the young people in their random sample would have been involved in offending.

10 cf the report 'Crime and the Family' (Utting, Bright and Henricson, 1993).

11 West (1982) showed that having a parent with a criminal record increased the likelihood of involvement in delinquency amongst their sample of young men.

12 Catan, Dennison and Coleman (1996), in their sample of over 4,000 young people from a wide range of backgrounds, found that communication with mothers was rated as more positive than with fathers.

Many young people were keen to reject any notion that they had suffered as a result of growing up in a one-parent family:

..the court tried to say 'maybe it's because he's in a one parent family'. Now to me that's not right, my mum's as good as any mum, just because she's on her own, I don't care what the judge says, I told him that. (Young man)

The majority felt that their parents had tried all they could to keep them from following deviant careers, encouraging them to remain in school and employing a range of disciplinary measures.

They used to beat me to keep me out of trouble
(Under 18 young man)

A: *I was just going into [name of shop] to pinch (...) and me parents took me to the police station*
A: *My mum stuck my picture round all the shops in [name of seaside town]*
A: *Never do it again*
Q: *Oh to stop you?*
A: *And when I was 13 she told all the shops 'don't serve her fags or booze'.*
Q: *Did it make any difference?*
A: *It was good...* (Young women)

She tried everything, tried everything and it's not worked has it? It's down to me at the end of the day, I know what's got to be done. They tear their hair out trying to help don't they? They try everything but at the end of the day it's down to you. (Young man)

Many young people felt strongly that no intervention on the part of their families could have made them desist.

There's nothing you can do to stop it, I've had some talks with me mum and no matter what she's said to me it hasn't changed me in the slightest. They can batter you all they want, they can sit down and talk to you sensibly all they want, but at the end of the day if you're going to do it nothing's going to stop you is it?

(Young man)

Several now regretted not listening to the warnings they had been given.

Some young people did offer insight into ways they felt their parents could have reached them. Improvements in communication were often central to this.

Like my dad was an ex-army man so I could never talk to him, he was proper strict, he didn't like me, I didn't like him.

(Young man)

The need for there to be discipline, ground rules, and for a child to receive attention from their parents was acknowledged.

Very few young people described being encouraged to commit crimes by their families.

I was brought up as a criminal, my dad had me out robbing for him when I was a kid, it's just been my way of life for years.

(Young man)

The areas that they grew up in: 'It's a lot to do with where you live'

A number of young people talked about the communities they had grown up in. They described estates with high levels of deprivation[13]. Drug use, unemployment, violence, and crime were extremely common[14].

...where I grew up there was fucking nothing, just riots all the time, shootings all the time, just violence all the time. I'd seen it all when I was a kid you know what I'm saying? (Young man)

Most of the families in the areas where they lived were seen to have only one parent:

...they go out and dump single parents in the same area. What I'm trying to say is where I used to live in [name of area], it's like a rough, nasty area and you just see mums with 6 children, 3 kids, their boyfriend, not a dad. Kids grow up and they grudge other families... (Young woman)

Many talked about an absence of any facilities for young people where they grew up.

Environment was seen by many of the young people to have strong impact on the route they had taken and their entry into crime.

I spent a little time around [name of seaside town] and [name of seaside town]...which is kind of a good area, but moving back to [name of Midlands town] again, back into council estates and I went back to me old self again.
(Young man)

13   Children's Express have carried out research looking at young people's experience of growing up in such areas (report to the Social Exclusion Unit, 1998).
14   Bright (1999) sees targetting high crime neighbourhoods as an essential part of the strategy to reduce youth crime.

Most believed that parents could do little to combat the negative influence of these estates.

What about all these rough areas in the big cities and that? There's nothing my mum can do to change that area is there? It's not her fault that I was brought up in that area is it? It's the government's fault for letting it get into such a bad state. Council houses with boards on the windows, it's down to the councils isn't it? (Young man)

Experiences of the care system: '...doesn't do nowt for you'

A large proportion of each group had experienced being in the public care system at some time whilst growing up. For some this had been periods when their parents were unable to deal with their difficult, or offending, behaviour.

She tried, she tried her hardest, but I was actually driving people mad in my family, pushing them to the brink, you understand. And my mum had to say 'I don't want to give my child away, but you'll have to take her away from me' because she had my sister and brother and she couldn't handle it, I was actually driving people mad and she had to give me away for them to give me some help. But now my mum regrets it and that because she thought that by telling social services to help me, my mum's African and that and she's got a really strong family sense and that, and it really hurt her to give me away, but she thought they were going to help me, and it really hurts her now because she brought them into the family, they took me away. I'm the only one who can say 'I was brought up in a children's home' in my family, and they never did anything because look at where I am now. (Young woman)

Many young people had been in care for long periods of their childhood. One young woman described herself:

I'm a social services baby yeah...I've got files that thick, if you want to know anything go to social workers about me, don't ask my mother nothing. (Young woman)

A number of young people described being passed from institution to institution, for example:

I've been to 6 schools, 2 boarding schools, 2 assessment centres, 2 secure units, 3 psychiatric places, 2..4 children's homes. (Under 18 young woman)

The young women we talked with were particularly incensed about their experiences. They described an absence of positive role models and supervision. They saw their route into crime as almost inevitable.

> *We've all been through social services, foster, children's homes, getting kicked out of school, secure unit...I'm sure we've all been through that road, it's like a journey and we've all collected our tickets along the way.* (Young woman)

Many young people, both male and female, commented on the relationships they had had with their social workers. They were divided on whether the relationships had been positive or negative for them. A number felt that they had been able to establish long-term links, even friendships, through which they had gained material and emotional support. This was particularly so for the under 18s we spoke to.

> A: *...social worker was good...When I was on the out she'd see me, take me out buy me clothes.*
> Q: *She didn't stop you getting back in though did she?*
> A: *She tried though, at least she tried...she tried to take me to youth clubs, I didn't like it but I went along with it because I thought she was safe, she was down to earth. She was trying to help.* (Young man)

Other young people had little positive to say. They had just limited contact with social workers who changed frequently. They felt that the individuals they had been in contact with had done little to help them and failed to honour promises. In some instances it was felt that the actions of social workers had even resulted in them being refused bail or receiving harsher sentences.

Several individuals raised the issue of a lack of continued support from the care system on reaching 16 or 18. They described how their needs for help in facing the transition from care to independent living went unmet[15]. The particular difficulties they described facing were around housing, sources of income, and managing finances.

> *I've been in care all me life since I was a baby, as soon as you reach 16 they kick you out and wipe their hands of you, so I was left in the big wide world with a 2 year old child thinking 'where am I going to go, what am I going to do?' and I couldn't get income support until I was 17, that's stupid, how am I supposed to feed a child? I had to go out there and do crime to feed myself, clothe my child, feed my child, plus I had a drug habit...* (Young woman)

---

15   The failure to help young people manage the transition from care to independent living is identified by Davis et al (1998) as a key target area for improvement.

They help you while you're in care, when I was in care they gave me like 37 quid a week, and I wasn't allowed to eat their scran I had to buy my own , to get us into the idea of buying your own food, cooking your own meals, buying your own washing powder, getting me ready for moving me into independent living accommodation. But it only helps while you're there, it's novelty, you think 'yeah' but once you get out it's like 'nah £37 a week' and you've got to pay bills and that out of that, and that hits you because you don't have to pay nothing like that when you're in care, electric bills, water rates, gas and all that. So when you get into accommodation on your own it hits you like a brick in the head.   *(Young man)*

Crime was often said to be a response to the need to gain money and materials for survival after being 'abandoned' by the care system.

Experiences of education: 'They just see problem child'

Many young people had had very limited contact with formal schooling. A small number had not attended school at any point in their lives. The majority had ended their involvement with mainstream schooling well before the school leaving age. The average age appeared to be around 14, but was as low as 11. An extremely common pattern seemed to be periods of frequent truanting and challenging behaviour particularly upon reaching secondary school age. It is interesting to note that no negative references were made to experiences at primary school.

Involvement with crime and substance abuse had sometimes taken place in school itself. Young people felt they had been more interested in 'messing about' rather than taking notice. They stated that they had 'better things to do' rather than attend school.

...the teachers they used to lock the classroom door and keep you there in detention for an hour, hour and a half...you don't want to be there as it is, let alone for another hour. Then you start to like it not going, you think 'this is good'. You get into the little nitty gritty things, behind the garden shed, smoking your drugs...
          (Young man)

Few young people felt that any of their teachers had had positive impact. In a number of instances the opposite was the case, the following is one extreme example:

Because I always got picked on by teachers, I used to have spelling difficulties and because I were always behind, they were pushing me too far, and in the end I took an overdose.   *(Young woman)*

A number of young people had received, often repeated, exclusions[16].

> *I was in school, I kept going back to school and coming out of school. In the end the teacher asked me to leave, just said 'don't come back'.* (Young man)

Following a series of expulsions many young people had fallen through the educational net. Other schools were unwilling to admit them. A number had been referred to specialist education units and others had been assigned home tutors. The input of home tutors was seen to be short lived and unhelpful.

> *...I was on bail for 8 months and about 3 weeks before I get sentenced, they send me a tutor! And they say 'yeah have a tutor, do it at home' but there's no point, I thought 8 months and they never done nothing, never come and see me and then for 2, 3 weeks* (Under 18 young man)

---

16   Both Graham and Bowling (1995) and the Audit Commission report 'Misspent Youth' (1996) demonstrate a link between regular truanting and school exclusion and involvement in offending.

Young Men and Education

The school I went to, like every day of the week there'd be something going off, big enquiries and all, if a coat went missing they'd ask you and all that. I just started getting into these little crowds, starting grafting all the time, taking coats, just robbing all the time. When I hit about 12, 13, I started drinking and that, started going off school, so they got the education out and said to me mum if he doesn't go to school we're going to charge you £1000. I said all right, and because I were bunking off that school they took me to another one, and they put me in this school that was miles and miles away from me area. So I just got down there one day and blew up arguing with me teacher and she said 'I don't think you're fit for any school'. Just let me out loose on the street.

She said what ?

'I don't think there's any school suitable for you' I was just ... at 9 o'clock I'd be on the streets all day, know what I'm saying? Grafting

Did anybody else have trouble staying...?

Me last school, the place where I lived, I was only there for a week and they kicked me out. I'd broke every rule within a week and then the week after that they took me back in and I were only there for (...) and they kicked me out again.

Did they give you chances, did they tell you?

No. After I got kicked out they just look down at you. You're just not fit for no school.

It annoyed me because I told them, 'yeah', that I do want to learn, and I don't see why I should do things that I've already done - read that thing and answer those questions. You go to school to learn yeah? So I'd just say to them: 'there's no point you giving me this work, I'm not learning anything'. If I'd have just said 'I'm not doing this work' they'd ignore me. But they said I wasn't fit for school, but I wanted to learn things, you go to school to learn.   (Young men)

A very small minority had remained in school up to the official leaving age and fewer still had gained qualifications. The groups expressed respect for those individuals who had. Many regretted that they did not work or stay on at school.

I've never ever sat a test, let alone an exam. I'd love to go back to school right now. Me mum used to say to me, I'd say 'I hate school' and she'd say 'I used to say that, but I wish I was at school, and you'll learn that when you're older' and now I have. Everything your mum says like that is true... (Young woman).

Gaining qualifications was seen to make life easier though it was acknowledged that it did not guarantee a future or employment.

Peer relationships: '...all the older boys, I looked up to them'

For many young people the peer group appeared to be of central importance. Debates around peer influence and peer pressure featured in most of the group discussions. Some young people took the view that much of their behaviour, including involvement with crime and drug use, had been in response to wanting to be like their friends and fit in with the peer group. Getting in with a 'bad' friendship group was given as explanation for involvement in crime [17].

Me, I've never been a criminal in me entire life, I've never done nothing stupid apart from, I only got one conviction. It was my friends that I hang round with, the group that I hang round with, I got influenced I went along with them and I got into trouble.
(Under 18 young man)

Several young people described wanting what their friends, particularly older friends, had and being introduced to ways of obtaining these desired objects.

...we all hang round the flats, and you'd have like your friends, the older boys, and every one'd be smoking puff and that, and you're thinking 'I want to be like them'- in their nice clothes, and then you find out how they're making the money, so you have a go, and you succeed, and you think 'that's easy'. (Young man)

A number of young people rejected the suggestion of peer group influence. Instead they gave choice and self determination as explanations for their behaviour:

At the end of the day your mates can't force you to do it, it's you isn't it, if you don't want to do it you don't want to do it... they can't shove it down your throat, it's up to you at the end of the day.
(Young man)

---

17   Graham and Bowling (1995) quantified the relationship between offending and peer delinquency. They found a strong positive correlation between the two, but were unable to conclude any causal relationship. It may be that offenders attract each other, supporting delinquency, but not causing it.

Involvement with drugs: 'It's just life, it's just normal'

A high proportion of the young people making up the groups had been involved with drugs before entering custody. Soft drug use was seen to be a 'normal', 'everyday' activity [18]:

> *You wake up and you have a spliff like you have a cup of tea.*
>
> *(Young man)*

As expected, cannabis was most frequently used. Heroin and crack cocaine were seen to be the main problem drugs. A substantial proportion of those in the groups had in the past, or immediately prior to entering custody, been involved with hard drugs. Involvement in crime had often emerged as a consequence of needing to support drug habits [19].

> *When you're a smackhead, it's the same thing: you go out, you rob, you graft, you sell your stuff, you score, you do the same every single day, nothing in your head, nothing, just that.* *(Young woman)*

Many young people had become involved with drugs from an early age. Explanations for beginning to use drugs, and escalating their use, included seeing friends and older young people using, and getting bigger highs. As discussed above, many young people lived in environments where drug use was extremely common and very visible. A small number discussed how they had experienced friends or family members overdosing, sometimes fatally.

For some drug use was an escape from the problems in their lives.

> *Like when we were little, I lived on me own, when I were 7 just me and me brother because me mum left, and he'd come in and I'd be crying. I used to sit there smelling me mum's coat, the smell of it and I'd be saying '[brother's name], I just want me mum' and he'd go like that 'come on it's all right, let's play a game, let's mess about, let's go and doss out', you know, to get me head out, and that's his way of coping with things, just pretend it's not there, take heroin and it goes away. That's why I couldn't come off it because every time I had a dig it took everything away.* *(Young woman)*

Many young people were eager to address their drug addictions. They acknowledged the destructive effects of drugs on their own lives and upon their families. Gaining access to help had often not been easy. Drug counselling, when available, was often seen to be ineffective as the

---

18 Parker et al (1995) further endorse this view, they suggested that drug use had now become 'normalized'.

19 Graham and Bowling (1995) concluded that young people involved in drugs and alcohol are likely to 'become embedded in a criminal lifestyle from which it becomes increasingly difficult to disengage from'.

counsellors have had little or no experience of their own with drugs. A number of young people felt that prison sentences for drugs offences were inappropriate; those with drug addictions need rehabilitation and treatment clinics rather than punishments.

Involvement with drinking: 'It were just one stupid thing, just pissed up'

References to excessive alcohol use also featured in the groups, though they were less central than discussions of drug use. Both young women and young men stated that drinking had prompted them to become involved in acts which were out of their character when sober: the main example of this was fighting [20].

> *I'd never been in trouble before or anything like that, never had a caution. Went out with me mate one night, had a good drink, walking down home we ended up fighting and I ended up here...if we'd have been sober we'd probably have walked the other way.*
> *(Young man)*

Drinking was seen to increase levels of aggressiveness and decrease a young person's ability to think about the consequences of their actions.

Young people's routes into being involved in crime: '...comes down to you'

Various explanations for involvement in activities which had resulted in them being in custody were offered. Some individuals gave a number of these explanations to account for their behaviour.

Some young people offered accounts which suggested they had seen crime as a way of obtaining what they desired. In some cases it was a preferred alternative to gaining legitimate employment.

> *With young people yeah, I'm not saying that they don't want to work or anything yeah, but as everyone knows it's the legal way to make money, and they just see that as they can't be bothered, they just ain't got no sense.*   *(Under 18 young man)*

For others, drug dependencies motivated their need to gain large sums of money on a regular basis.

---

20   Rutter, Giller & Hagell (1998) reviewed research and concluded that excessive alcohol use increased the likelihood of involvement in violent acts.

For some crime supplied the money they felt they needed for survival, for example to supplement inadequate benefit payments.

A small number of young people explained their involvement in crime as a search for a 'buzz'.

> *...it was the buzz, the adrenaline, when I first started I was shaking and that fucking shitting meself, like going round the back gardens, back of houses and that... but it just used to become a habit...*
>
> (Young man)

Delinquent peer groups were given as explanation by a small number of young people. Many of these individuals now regretted their involvement with such groups.

One young person described involvement with triad gangs that had necessitated him being involved in dangerous and criminal activities.

A number of young people did not see themselves as 'criminals'. Their involvement in physical fighting had been due to excessive alcohol intake or by the need to defend themselves. Pubs, clubs and the streets were the places where this was most likely to take place. Many young people, young women included, felt a strong need to defend themselves from any attack. It was seen as unthinkable to walk away from an attack on them or a threat.

A small number of young people suggested that the desire for attention motivated involvement with crime in some individuals, though not themselves.

> *...most of it's attention seeking. Like going out robbing a car, it's just to get caught, maybe try and get a bit of a name for themselves. They want a bit of attention so that people care about them.*
>
> (Young man)

Notions of choice and self-determination seemed to be at the root of discussions accounting for how young people became involved with offending. Many had had people in their lives, particularly family, who had tried to prevent them becoming involved in crime. These warnings were ignored; efforts to make them stop and think were not successful.

> *But you know our fault is that we stop and think once we've done it, take him out and then think 'oh I shouldn't have done that really', you think at the wrong time.* (Young man)

Young people described their attitudes:

...it comes down to you at the end of the day, you're going to be the one that's going to stop you, because no matter what they say, they ain't going to stop you. It's just in one ear, out the other when they're talking to you.   *(Young man)*

Young Women and Fighting

I was showing off in front of loads of boys, that's why I was doing it. I thought I was big and hard but I wasn't. Because we never won fights - you won fights didn't you? I'd never ever do it again, all this I've had to go though, and I've had it. I've been jumped.

I had a reason, I don't know how to say about it but this lass told me that (...) and she thought (...) and she ended up in the gutter, and then I came and smacked her. And I'd do it again because she deserved everything she got, and she got nothing.

Yeah but miss, you know when I fighted that lass, when I got home my sister battered me for doing that

Do you think that's fair enough?

But I got worse than what she got!

My mam sat down and talked to me about it, she didn't pop at me, she didn't. I, she didn't hit me or owt because hitting me wouldn't do nowt, and kicking off at me wouldn't do nowt for me, it would just make me and me mum argue. So she sat down and talked about it and that. She were disappointed, which is right innit? But she didn't kick off at me or hit me or scream and shout at me or owt like that, she knows that wouldn't do no good for me.

You know I've been grown up right, if someone comes to me and hits me I'm not allowed to back down, I have to hit them. But I'm not allowed to start no fight, you know what I mean? I'm not allowed to start no fight, if I start any fight then I'm going to get battered meself. But if I get battered then I'm going to get her battered again off me mum. But if I start a fight then, you know what I mean...

You've got to be able to look after yourself, don't take no crap but don't go round..

Many of the young people felt strongly that they had to make their own mistakes, that they could not learn from those of others, but that they had to experience things for themselves. Their involvement could only stop when they felt the time was right.

Involvement with the police: 'They take advantage of their power'

Questions regarding perceptions of the police stirred up strong animated responses, most especially amongst the young men we spoke to. With just a few exceptions the police were perceived negatively. They were seen to 'hassle' young people out on the streets[21]; to let their uniform 'go to their head'; and to abuse their power. With regard to communication, the police were seen to talk down to young people and to see themselves as superior[22].

Many felt that the police had been eager for them to offend, as part of a point scoring exercise or part of a game; and that the police had tried to set them up or manipulate their accounts.

> *Walking around the street now, and like I've been arrested before yeah for a theft and I were stitched up by the police, and a burglary. I was walking down the street in the town centre, a busy day, and the police pulled me over, and I put me hands up, and they said 'get in the back of the van' so I got in and the police hit me and they said right grab hold of that screwdriver, (...) they wanted me to look like I'd been breaking into a car.* (Young man)

A number of young people described instances of police violence. The consensus seemed to be that such acts were common. Young people felt that complaints procedures were not open to them as they felt they were unlikely to be believed because of their record. Several black young people raised the issue of police racism. They felt that they, members of their family, and their communities, were particularly likely to be abused, both verbally and physically, by the police:

> *I think back to the time when they arrested my dad, they beat him up, shouted racial abuse at him, and it was only because my mum and dad had a little argument that the police got called, it weren't really nothing serious, but the way they treated my dad, like he was some kind of animal. They tried to suffocate him...* (Under 18 young man)

---

21   Research by Reiner (1992) offers empirical support for this view point in young males.
22   This coincides with research that shows young people, generally, are critical of the police and their approach to communication (Catan, Dennison and Coleman, 1996).

Young Men and the Police

When I was 15 they [the police] used to rag me about all the time man. They rag everybody about

They rag most people about, but are they going to rag your old man about? No man I don't think they are. Two coppers come up to an old man and grab hold of him they'll probably say 'come on such and such, let's have you' and put you in the car. With me it's like 'In the fucking car' Bam. That's what it used to be, you don't see them doing that with a big grown...

Have people spent any time in police cells?

Yeah.

Everybody here

Every time I get locked up, because they know I'm an addict, and I need me medicine sort of thing, they always go for a three day local, try and crank me up to say 'yeah I've done this, yeah I've done that'. And it's got to the stage now where I know the time I'm locked up I'm either not getting out and going straight to jail, or I'm staying in for 3 days and then going out.

I have to just keep me mouth shut and ride them 3 days out. I'd prefer to do an extra 3 month in here than I would to do 3 days in a police station, anytime.

They're shit them police cells. It's just a little cell.

Is the treatment different, the policeman's treatment to the prison officer's treatment?

Yeah

In what kind of way?

'You little bastard shut up'

(Young men)

One or two young people gave examples of times when the police had helped them. One young man described police intervention in a domestic incident.

> *A: They know where you're coming from, if you have a domestic at home and your mum don't want you living there and she calls the police or something, I've been in those situations, do you know what I'm saying... you have an argument and the police come and you think 'fuck, my mum just called the police on me'. And you think to yourself 'right' and you're trying to explain yourself to the police and the police know where you're coming from and you're trying to calm your mum down and calm you down. It is embarrassing but they know what you're going thorough because they deal with you and you're not the first person they've had to deal with.*
>
> *Q: So when that happened to you they did it quite well ?*
>
> *A: Yeah, they did deal with it well. They calmed me old girl down, they calmed her down and they told me to go out for a little while and then come back after, and when I come back after me mum was calmed down and we talked through it again. Do you know what I'm saying, we managed to get on with things, it is quite good.   (Young man)*

More commonly young people felt they had been treated 'okay' by *some* individuals on *some* occasions.

> *...it depends who you get (...). You can get the ones who treat you fairly, not good, but treat you fairly.   (Under 18 young man)*

However, the majority of young people did not have respect for the police. Nor did they see them as any deterrent against becoming involved in crime.

Experiences of the courts: 'It just depends on the judge...what sort of day he's having'

Many of the young people were angry at the treatment they had received from the courts. They felt that there had been no understanding of their backgrounds or upbringing. Judges were seen to be drawn from privileged backgrounds, with little understanding of what these young peoples' lives are like.

> *If you give a judge one day, like a whole day from morning to night in my area he'd understand where you're coming from. There's no way, I reckon he'd end up smoking crack mate! I know it sounds funny but it's serious because the way people are, like you'll see someone selling crack on that corner, then halfway down the street there's somebody else.   (Young man)*

Magistrates were seen to possess little, neither qualifications nor experience, that qualified them to sit in judgement:

> *A bunch of fucking shopkeepers sending you to jail, (...) that's all they are, civil servants. Shopkeepers, bank clerks, grannies, granddads, they sit there and send you to jail and ruin your life, bollocks (...) how the fuck can they preach? They're just normal people off the streets, you know what I mean...18 months in prison from shopkeepers.*   *(Young man)*

Judges and magistrates were also seen to pay little attention to pre-sentence reports. A number of young people interpreted their behaviour as not 'caring'.

Many young people felt that the courts were extremely inconsistent in the sentences they passed[23]. They felt that other prisoners or their co-defendants had received significantly higher or lower sentences for very similar crimes, even considering their previous records.

Sentences were seen to be dependent on the judge's mood that day. Race was also seen to be a factor that resulted in inconsistent sentencing, with black young people believing that they received harsher sentences[24]. Young women also believed that the courts were prejudiced against them[25], they believed they were treated more severely, as criminal activity was seen to be inappropriate behaviour for women of any age.

The justice system was not only seen to be biased but also incompetent. Some young people described examples of errors which had worked against them, for example:

> *When we were in the court they stood up and read my name, and they read all her [co-defendant's] background, and I'd never been in trouble before but it looked dead bad. I've never been in trouble before and they're saying all shop robberies....*
>   *(Under 18 young woman)*

Long drawn out procedures involving a series of adjournments before final sentencing were also seen to be a common experience[26].

Attitudes to non-custodial outcomes: 'It's just like getting away with it'

Non custodial sentences were discussed by only a small number of the groups, the reason being that few young people stated that they had received

---

23   Rutter, Giller & Hagell (1998) review research on court outcomes for young people and conclude that disparity of outcomes across geographical areas and groups continues to be a feature despite recent initiatives.

24   Research by Hood (1992) revealed that those from minority ethnic groups were treated more harshly by the courts.

25   Hedderman & Gelsthorpe (1997) found that women and men were treated differently by the courts but not necessarily more leniently or more harshly.

such outcomes. Instead they had been sent to prison for their first offence. Many young people felt they had not been offered a 'second chance'.

Cautions were not taken seriously, as in the following comments:

.   *they're nothing really, they're a telling off.*   (Young man)

It's just like getting away with it.   (Young man)

Of those who had received community service orders, or had a view of them, there was a mix of attitudes as to their effectiveness in preventing further involvement in crime and their desirability as a consequence of a court appearance. Some young people felt they were effective because they impacted on their life in the community, rather than removing them from it. They worked because they caused embarrassment:

...it works, because you think to yourself 'oh I don't want to do that, make myself look like a mug again'.   (Young man)

Others were less positive; they were angered by having to work without pay and, therefore, wherever possible, did not attend. It was felt that they learnt little from their involvement and gained little rehabilitation:

Community service you don't learn bollocks mate, sweeping the floor? How are you going to learn not to pinch, like me I am addicted to pulling handbags...   (Young woman)

Contact with probation before entering custody: 'Every time you've got a different person to see'

Probation services, like other professional groups in contact with young offenders in the community, were thought to offer little help or support. With one or two exceptions, young people said that their probation officer did not care about them or do much for them.

...he didn't give a shit. They're lazy...   (Young man)

As long as they're getting paid they'll just sit there and chat.
          (Under 18 young man)

Some young people thought that it was difficult to make any sort of relationship with probation staff because of the high turnover of individuals assigned to work with them. As they grew older, several found the transition from youth justice to probation staff hard to handle.

When I was younger they put me on a supervision order where you have to see...youth justice workers. And I used to see her like once a week...and I could talk to her about my problems and that... She was alright, she was not like these probation officers where you don't see them... when they get hold of you, they don't seem to care. It's like as if to say - make your own way in life because you're not young any more, you should make your own mind up.

(Young man)

While some young people endorsed the idea of support in the community, most were critical of what was on offer in practice.

Young Men and Problems with the System

They stitch you up as well. I know someone, I won't mention his name like, but someone I know in here, and he got about 4 years for armed robbery, did his time and he got out, got parole. And he got a job and everything, he was getting on with his life, a good job and he was trying to get on with his life, but he missed one appointment, breached it, and they brought him back here. I think that's pathetic. For someone that's tried hard, that's got a job for themselves, trying their best, just one little slip up and they bring him back. I think that's bad that.

The probation officer doesn't know what's going on. They should know you - they're your probation officer. They should know that you're going down again - they should know what's happening in your life shouldn't they? But you can just turn up there any day of the week pissed up, tell them a load of shite and walk out the door again. They don't know any different do they? It shouldn't be that way should it? And then you get arrested, you're in court in the cells and he comes to see you 'I thought you were doing all right again'. Pub...

I put a claim in against probation with me solicitors, because they - I got arrested, they said I'd breached me bail but I'd finished it, and I finished it over a year ago. And they said they were sending me letters, and they knew where I was living but I ain't got no letters or nothing. And I got picked up and arrested and put in the cells for 2 nights, and when I did go to court they realised that they'd make a mistake. So I've got a claim in now for that

What's your experience of going through the courts?

Well I've been to court one time, [name of court] Crown, and the judge yeah, Judge [name] he's called, and he's got a problem that guy. He was late. I was made to wait about 3 hours because they took me in the holding cells before I went up and they said 'He's not here yet - he's at the golf course - he forgot he's supposed to be at work'. He must have got into trouble over it, but it's things like that. They don't care do they. He probably thought 'get it over and done with, get back to playing golf or summat, send him down'. They should take more notice of your pre-sentence reports as well, because they don't. I got a pre-sentence report for me, they don't, they just turn a blind eye don't they? They don't look at your background or anything. (Young men)

In summary, the young people we spoke to offered few examples of professionals having a positive impact on their lives. This view seems to hold true of their experiences in custody.

3 Being in Prison

To find out how they perceived their everyday lives in prison young people were asked to focus on a number of specific issues. These included: how it felt to arrive in prison for the first time; what they felt about reception and induction; their relationships with staff, and how these could be improved; relations between prisoners; aspects of education or offending behaviour programmes they felt may have been helpful; and any positive and negative effects of prison.

The young people responded from their own personal perspectives and also talked about the experiences of their friends and relatives. They held strong opinions. Two primary concerns emerged clearly from the groups. First, that most young people did not think they were treated in a way appropriate to their needs or their age[27]. Second, that prison was a dislocating experience for the majority. It was a 'whole other life', not connected to their everyday lives before entering custody, and often not preparing them at all well for release back into the community.

First impressions of prison: '...treated like rubbish, treated like rubbish'[28]

There was a marked difference between young people's first ever impression of coming into prison and their subsequent comparative experiences.

First time experiences were mixed. The majority of young women and young men felt degraded and alienated.

Horrible, scared   *(Under 18 young woman)*

When you come in, they take you off the van, they tell you to come into that little room and you've got to walk fast, here and there, get yourself dressed and everything. And then you go get your food, get banged up, and as you go in there, there's an atmosphere, all the boys asking for cigarettes and that.   *(Under 18 young man)*

---

27 See Hayman (1998)
28 The particular needs of young people coming into custody are noted in 'Young Prisoners: A Thematic Review' (HM Chief Inspector of Prisons, 1997).

A: *Humiliated... do you know, like, they were telling me to take my knickers off.*
Q: *Knickers off?*
A: *Like strip searched*
A: *It shames you*
A: *It's embarrassing*
A: *You just feel like a catalogue delivery, like you're nothing. 'Here's your delivery', that's it and you're just given a number...*
A: *I felt disgusted. I did, I'm not joking.*   (Young woman)

Others had found that things were not as bad as imagination or rumour had led them to expect. Many believed that prison would be a place where they would be raped or attacked and it was almost a relief that it was less intimidating than they had imagined.

A: *My first impression of prison was a grin, because I thought it was about twenty times worse that it really is...*
A: *I expected to see people hanging themselves and stuff, having to be a big bad man to be prepared to fight everyone...*
                                             (Under 18 young man)

I thought it were going to be like that film 'Scrubbers'
                                             (Under 18 young woman)

The first night was the worst.

My first time in jail, when I first come in, I was like 'woooooaaaaah'. You look at everything and you think 'is this what it's like then?' All the stories that you've heard and now you've finally found out. You don't really think much of it 'til you're behind your door and you're like that - man - thinking 'Nah man, 8 o'clock at night, you're behind your door. And you're like 'No shit. I'm in jail - man'...It kicks you in the head when you first come in.
                                             (Young man)

When I first came here I were a bit frightened at first, a bit paranoid...it took me about 2 months to settle in properly.
                                             (Young man)

Young people who moved from closed to open establishments found a marked contrast.

A: *You get used to the closed system and you come here and you see everyone walking around on their own...*

A: It's totally different from what you've just come from. You've just come from not being able to move or not do anything...

A: My mate told me all about it and I didn't believe him at first, you know, you have your own key and all this and I said "No you're pulling my leg".   (Young man)

Although they did not devote a great deal of time to its discussion, most young people seemed to think that the induction procedure had been of only limited help to them. One person said 'It's a joke'. A number felt that they had been given insufficient information when they first came into the prison. Many had had to rely on guesswork with regard to regimes' practice such as making bedpacks or specific establishment rules[29]. A considerable number said that much of the induction period was spent behind their doors.

I've just come here right and I've done an induction thing, and like for the last 3 days...I've been to the gym once, and since then I've been asking to go to the gym...I've been banged up in my cell all week.   (Under 18 young man)

On your first day yeah, they put you behind your door and give you a pack and then in the morning they come in and say 'what you doing in bed?' How are you supposed to know that you're supposed to get up, make your bed, get all your covers off and fold them at the end of the bed?   (Under 18 young woman)

Well, obviously, I've had my induction programme a few times in here but they never once told me I could do my GCSEs, never once. I only found it out on this sentence.   (Young man)

*I thought it were alright, I thought it helped.
                    (Under 18 young woman)*

Child or adult?: 'We are still kids'

Many of the young people were critically aware of what it meant to be growing up in prison. They talked about whether they saw themselves as a child or as an adult. They spoke of how, in many ways, they had had to 'grow up' fast.

I'm 17 on Sunday but I know I'm quite old for my age. (Young man)

Big as we think we are, and even though I am the mother of a 5 year old child, we are still kids. We might think that we're women but deep down we are teenagers still. Because people say to me

---

29   Such views strongly support the recommendations for the Induction programme cited in HM Chief Inspector of Prisons Thematic Review (1997).

'you've got a child, why ain't you grown up properly?' But at the end of the day I was a baby who had a baby. I'm still an 18 year old girl[30]. (Young woman)

They spoke frankly about how they saw themselves and how they felt they were positioned by others.

> A: *Cracking jokes and that. Staff don't realise what they're doing because we're younger. They'd be better cracking a joke with a con than a YO.*
>
> Q: *Do you think they've got a thicker skin or something?*
>
> A: *Yeah, well, they wouldn't take it to heart so much would they? You get people a lot younger, they just crumble, they can't handle it.* (Young man)

They've got in my file that I'm childish. And I went to sentence planning and he says 'are you childish?' I said 'No' because I'm a loud person me, I like to have a laugh and that, I don't like sitting being morbid. So they put in my file that I'm childish and I'm only 17. But they're going to get that behaviour aren't they, because I am a child. They should understand that when they're sending us all to prison. (Under 18 young woman)

Young people were critical of the way they were treated by prison staff because of their age.

I don't like the way they speak to you. Like because you're a younger offender, you're a little kid. They've all worked in cons' prison where they've been a nobody, they've kept their mouth shut…And then they come here and suddenly they're working with a load of kids that they can shout at and they talk down to you. (Young man)

They keep saying 'this place is full of kids, all of yous are children'. But at the end of the day, if someone's playing pool, taking a shot and the pool ball comes off the table, someone kicks the ball – that's it – the whole of the wing is banned from playing pool for a week. I said to them – they treat us like school kids – not allowed to play pool for a week? – and then you're telling us that we act like kids. So – if they were saying to us 'you're 20 years old, you don't need to be kicking the pool ball on the floor, why do it?'. Not just banned you for a week. People think 'you treat us like school children – we'll act like school children'. (Young man)

Many young people thought that officers displayed conflicting expectations.

---

30   Caddle and Crisp (1997) found that women in prison had a high incidence of very early pregnancy and childbirth

On the one hand young people were expected to behave like adults (which they felt they were not) and, on the other, they were not given the same facilities or treatment as adult prisoners, because they were seen as children.

> *You're an adult when they want you to be, you're a child when they want you to be.* (Young woman)

Young people often felt compromised, obliged to cope with officers teasing them or repeatedly 'turning over' their cells, when in reality they felt such behaviour to be exploiting an officer's position of power.

> *They say there's bullies on the unit and that but the screws are bullying people as well, you know. They're causing people distress as well. They have a go at people more than anyone else. They just don't see it like that.* (Young man)

Relationships with staff: 'I'm not saying no officer's safe, but some are safer in some ways'

Although there were some individual instances of good rapport with officers, almost all young people felt that they had an uneasy or at best tenuous relationship with prison staff at all levels. Many felt that officers saw their role as custodians rather than as carers.

> *As far as they're concerned they're just paid to open your door and let you out and then bang you back up.* (Young man)

Others felt that there was an abuse of power.

> *They like to have the authority to bang us up - the power to close the door in your face.* (Under 18 young man)

> *They think 'I've got the key so you just do what I say' - that's what they think.* (Under 18 young woman)

> *They love to see you getting nicked...when they give you the nicking sheet, there's smiles on their faces.* (Young man)

Some young people said that prison officers saw their role entirely negatively.

> *I think they're more interested in punishing you rather than helping you, there's no rehabilitation here... You're entitled to your meals, your association and that's about it.* (Young man)

Because I'm two year, I get called like from officers who know about me, like they've read my reports and the only things that get put down are bad things, you get me? Like the only thing that gets written down are nickings, and every so often something good will get written down but mainly it's the things you do wrong that you get noticed for.   *(Under 18 young man)*

Some of them have just got bad attitudes and you're asking them things and they just take no notice of you and they speak down to you, not like speaking to you, down to you just because you're in jail and that, because you're scum, just because you're in jail and that.   *(Young man)*

Most young people believed that prison officers should have a caring role.

They're here to look after us   *(Young man)*

Some felt that officers should be specifically trained to work with young people[31].

They should have staff like care workers that are trained for it, you know like in children's homes.   *(Under 18 young woman)*

The predominant view expressed regardless of age or gender was that some prison officers were 'alright' while others were not. The criteria for 'alright' seemed to be giving a straight answer or treating a prisoner with respect.

I like the ones that are straightforward, they're the best ones.   *(Under 18 young man)*

The ones I respect more are the ones that go by the book but have a laugh and a joke with...   *(Young man)*

You know what makes a good screw is when he tells you straight, doesn't hold punches 'here you are boss can you do me a favour and get such and such' and he says 'I can't', instead of some of them saying 'I'll get you it in 5 minutes' and half an hour later you'll ask them again and they'll say '5 minutes'. One that'll say stuff like that and never do it, or one that'll say straight 'I'm sick of your attitude' or say 'I've put your name in your book for such and such, I've given you a warrant in your book'. Half of them just put your name down and don't even tell you.   *(Young man)*

---

31   These views support the recommendations of the Youth Justice Board regarding staff training and reflect the observations made in the Chief Inspector's Thematic Review. They are also born out in the focus of the TSA training pack 'The Nature of Adolescence' (1994, 1998) and TSA' current work to develop an accredited training programme for staff in secure settings.

The concept of mutual respect seemed to be of utmost importance.

> *Respect. If we respect them, they'll respect us, that's how it should be innit?* (Young man)

> A: *Good staff won't tell you to do something, they'll ask you to do something.*
> A: *'Please don't leave that bucket hanging there' and you go 'All right then'. But another would go 'do that now'.*
> (Young woman)

Dealings with individual officers seemed sometimes to be quite positive although there were mixed feelings about the relevance of the personal officer scheme. A number of young people found it difficult to sustain meaningful relationships with their personal officer.

> A: *We're supposed to work closely with staff on the [name] Wing because we've got an individual officer for each inmate, but it doesn't work like that. I haven't seen my personal officer for about 7 months…*
> A: *I haven't seen mine since I come here.* (Young woman)

Some felt that it was preferable to speak to someone else.

> *Mine's [name of officer]. I've never sat down and spoken to her about anything but [name of another officer] I've taken my personal letters to, that my dad's wrote to me… and she really helped me.*
> (Young woman)

Others felt that the only option was to deal with things themselves.

> *Our personal officer is just, oh I won't say it, but I won't talk to him. If I had a problem I won't go and see him, so I just have to keep it to myself, you know what I mean, cos, cos of his attitude towards us, towards me, I won't go and speak to him* (Young man)

A small minority felt that their personal officer had been helpful.

> *The only person that's helped me out since I've been in jail is my personal officer, and that's it.* (Young man)

Some young people serving long sentences felt that officers gave them little support with regard to their long-term plans.

I've been here like 2 years and I've never been taken in an office to talk to an officer - for him to say to me 'look do this'. You're supposed to do a sentence plan once you're convicted, and I've been here 2 years and they haven't even talked to me about a sentence plan. I haven't talked to an officer. I haven't been in the office once to talk to him.   *(Under 18 young man)*

Overall, many seemed resigned about the relationship between staff and prisoners.

A: *Some officers are strict, some are laid back. It depends on the officer doesn't it...*

A: *Whoever's on the wing at the time, if you've got a safe bunch then it's all right, if you haven't then you're fucked.*

A: *The majority of the officers - they're just moany old people that have been here for years.*   *(Young men)*

A considerable number of young people had little positive to say about governors.

Q: *What about the governor here, the governing governor, do you ever see him?*

A: *Can't trust him.*   *(Under 18 young man)*

Some spoke of the perceived lack of involvement of governors in their lives.

You never see the governor, apart from when he's walking round.   *(Young man)*

A: *You see them walking round and that...*

A: *They come and inspect your pad*   *(Young man)*

I think in closed [prisons] the governors only visit, they don't stay in prisons   *(Young man)*

Others felt that their close involvement with management might be construed negatively by other prisoners.

A: *If you're going to see the governor you must be giving names*

A: *It's when the officers tell everybody that you want to see the governor - starts rumours and that.*   *(Young man)*

Some governors, however, were visible and thought of in more positive ways.

Q: *What about the governor himself, do you ever see him?*
A: *He's sound...A lot of the officers don't like him because they say*
        he's too inmate-friendly   (Young man)

The governor called me into his office, sat me down, he goes 'Look
[name], forget that I'm the governor, what is your problem, how can
I help you?'   (Young woman)

Young people also had mixed feelings about other professionals that they
encountered while they were in prison.

Education: 'Give education their due, they're different, they're not prison'

In contrast to their experiences of mainstream education, many of the young
people we spoke with approached prison education in quite positive ways[32].

Well, you're going to need references and qualifications, so you might
as well do something while you're in jail.   (Young man)

A number felt that they had benefited from education.

I've already got two certificates - maths and English - and it doesn't
say prison, it says college.   (Under 18 young woman)

Views were also expressed that education could be an end in itself

Like at the moment, at the end of this year, I will have done 5 GCSEs
when I've been in here. I've come in with nothing. But I don't really
personally do them to like get a job or to help me get a job - I'm
doing it for meself, you understand.   (Under 18 young man)

But young people in prison were all too well aware that qualifications gained
could only be seen in perspective to the rest of their lives, often being
overshadowed by a criminal record or in their efforts to survive after release.

What's the point of getting all those qualifications if you're going to
come straight back in?   (Young man)

Their experiences highlighted many of the problems encountered by prison
education departments. Some young people were frustrated by the
imposition of prison regimes and policy on their attendance.

---

32   These views are upheld in the aims of the European Prison Educators Association (1998).

A: They have so many lock-downs and this, that and the other, you can't get to finish nothing...

A: Short-staffed, I think, that's one of the main problems isn't it? Short-staffed.   (Young men)

They do try and help you but they haven't got the equipment or half the things   (Young woman)

When I came here I was taking my GCSEs, they moved me a month before I was about to take my exams. I came here and when I came here I was on bang-up, like no education because I was on induction, so I missed it all out.   (Young man)

Others felt they had not been given adequate information as to what was on offer.

Q: Can you do stuff in here like courses and qualifications?

A: Yeah, you can do courses, there's different things NVQs and things like that...do your GCSEs...

A: I've only just found that out, no-one told me anything about it. I only found out about it in the last few weeks. They should let you know these things when you first come in (Young man)

Some young people found that their experiences of prison education staff reinforced their views on the inappropriateness of education to their lives in general.

Education...I tell you, down education there, I know more than half of them fucking teachers, half of them haven't got a clue. They teach you kids stuff anyway. They'll do some thing like division on the board – and she did it wrong and then tried to tell me I was wrong. Where does she get to be a teacher...When I came here, they gave me like a piece of paper with a story on it, no full stops, none of them punctuation marks, no commas no nothing in it. I had to put them in. I just looked round – you know what I mean – that's kids' stuff.
*   (Young man)*

But predominantly their views were reflected by that of one young woman who emphasised that going to education was less like being in prison:

In education they don't treat you like a prisoner as well – they treat you like you're in college.   (Under 18 young woman)

Links to outside probation, however, tended to reflect those experienced by young people prior to coming to prison.

Probation and other specialist services: 'What can they do for you?'

Overwhelmingly, young prisoners felt that they were poorly supported by outside probation services while they were in prison, saying that most probation staff retained little contact with the young people in their care.

A: *The last time I saw my probation officer was March…*
A: *She's done nothing…*
A: *I've seen mine twice in 13 months…*   (Young men)

Many young people reported that they had had a considerable number of changes in their personal probation officer.

I've been in jail 2 year and I've had about 10 different probation officers.   (Young man)

I just got a letter off her saying that she's been sacked and I'm having a new one.   (Young man)

Others felt that outside probation staff had little empathy with the young person's situation.

What can they do for you? They can't do nowt for you, they just sit there and take notes. They don't do nothing for you.(Young man)

You've read that letter from my probation haven't you? Writing to tell me about her holiday. Fuck off, I'd just been sentenced.
                                                        (Young woman)

Many felt neglected and unsupported.

If they were bothered about you, they'd come and see you every couple of months instead of leaving it 'til you get out. (Young man)

I got me mum to ring her up when I got me mum on a visit and she said to my mum that she can't come and see me until she's got about 3 or 4 to see in the jail. So in other words she's not coming in just to see me.   (Young man)

Positive experiences seemed to be much more the exception than the rule.

Mine sends me cards and postal orders, she goes to my mum's house and sees if me mum and me son are all right.   (Young woman)

Although most young people spoke negatively about probation and there was no specific reference to psychology in the prison setting they were positive about areas of the prison in which these professionals were involved, such as courses and groupwork.

They did, however, make direct reference to pastoral carers and those who mentioned the chaplaincy invariably spoke well about them.

> A: *He's the one person I've got respect for in the prison is the Chaplain, he's safe.*
> A: *When he's speaking he understands what you're saying and he listens.*   *(Under 18 young men)*

Some people, however, felt there were difficulties caused by age and experiential differences.

> *Yeah, but you're talking to people who are like 70 year old. They don't know half the stuff you're on about.*   *(Young man)*

Courses: 'Cognitive skills, that helped you a lot'

Certain aspects of the regime such as thinking skills and anger management courses were often supported by young prisoners[33] .

> *The way they deal with the MCs, the murder charges, they do do good for them... the way they have their discussions about things like the crimes, what provoked it and things like that, a lot of boys have calmed down since the discussions. Certain things like before they would just go off their head and start fighting. To talk about things and get things off your system, it is better for you I reckon.*
> *(Young man)*

> *I've done the thinking skills and it helps, seeing things from people's points of views. I know it's helped me.*   *(Young man)*

> A: *Yeah, I've been on an offending behaviour course...and I think that it done one of the best things for me, to be honest. One of the best things I've ever done in prison...*
> A: *Cognitive skills, that helped you a lot, that made you think. Cognitive skills - they say people only do that for parole but I done that as well, and it makes you think, it is helpful.*
> *(Young men)*

Others felt however that the course scenarios were inappropriate.

---

33   Accredited offending behaviour programmes designed to target criminogenic needs have been found to be effective when integrated into regimes as a whole (Goldblatt & Lewis,1998).

*A: I've done anger management in secure...they don't do
       anything like that in this prison...*
*A: It doesn't work anyway. All they say to you is take a deep
       breath - deep breaths and count to 10...*
A: You get your face smacked in - take deep breaths!!
                                                    (Young man)

*They say fill it in truthfully because there are no right or wrong
answers. Because if one of the questions is 'You walk into a pub and
someone's chatting up your girlfriend, what would you do?'
everybody, near enough everybody's put 'I'd go over and box the lad
out' So what they try and do is make you think the other side, see if
you can handle it any other way...What do they expect you to do,
buy him a pint?*   *(Young man)*

People talked a lot about the effects of alcohol in relation to their crimes and
tended to think that the alcohol awareness courses were useful when available.

*I'll do a drugs and an alcohol course because I drunk a lot on the
out, but they're the only courses I want to do... I was a heavy
drinker on the out yeah, and they showed us this video, that's what
made me think. And the drugs ones, you just see people fucked up off
drugs, losing arms and legs from fucking injecting - none of that for
me mate.*   *(Young man)*

*We used to have Alcoholics Anonymous in here, in the chapel, I used
to go.*   *(Young man)*

Some people were unconvinced of the relevance of courses to their long-
term plans.

*You can take a course in here, but when you get out you're going to
want to forget about this place, you're going to want to forget about
the course.*   *(Young man)*

A number felt that they were coerced into participation when courses were
linked to sentence planning or parole.

*About 3 weeks ago I got my sentence plan. This is my seventh prison
sentence. I said to them 'I'm not doing nothing'. So I got threatened with
getting time added on because I wouldn't participate in none of the
courses that the governors wanted me to do, so it's all shit. I've done
them all before on other sentences. They're not going to change me now
are they, if they never changed me then? I've done them in every jail I've
been to and they've done nothing for me. I don't intend to waste my time
and other people's by sitting through them all again.*   *(Young man)*

The experience of prison itself: 'You've got a different life innit – a whole other life'

Although the establishments and mix of young people was very diverse, there were a number of threads of discussion and interest which ran across all their prison experiences. Most young people saw prison as a separate world, disconnected from their lives outside. Once inside it they felt they developed an insight into how things really were in the establishment. They had little confidence that others, even the Inspectorate, gained a true picture.

> *It's not like they make it out to look like. Because I've seen it when inspectors come round the prison, everything sort of fixes up. That's all they'll show you, the inspectors don't know what's actually happening. This place is fucked up, excuse my language, but it is.*
> *(Under 18 young man)*

Young people gave widely differing appraisals of prison life. Many felt that prison had, in some ways, been a positive experience for them and were appreciative of the fact it had given them 'time to think' or 'get their heads sorted'.

> *I'd like to get locked up for 4 weeks, just to clean me head up and like have a fresh start.* *(Young man)*

> *I think it takes something like coming to jail to stop me coming into jail.* *(Young woman)*

> A: *I didn't think I was any good at art and that but I made some art sculptures and they were all right...*
> A: *Writing, I never wrote a single letter before I was in jail...*
> A: *I never wrote a letter before I came to jail either, but I could read and write. Reading as well. I hadn't read a book before.*
> *(Young man)*

Some young people believed that the sheer length of their sentence would prevent them from re-offending. This was especially so amongst those already serving substantial sentences. A number of these young people felt that this had given them time to think and made them more determined not to return.

> *I've been in a few times, this is my last time and the only reason this is me last time is because I've got a big sentence this time and it's knocked me into shape. I don't want this no more. (Young man)*

> A: *It's not until you get a really heavy sentence that you realise.*
> A: *Yeah you realise that life's more important.*

> *A: When you get life that's like the maximum sentence they can give you*
>
> *A: When you're in a local jail, then it's all fun and games, then you get 6 months, it's quick item then you're out–you get 6 months, you've probably already done 3 months, so you're out...When you get with a nine then you've got time to sit in your cell and think about it.* (Young men)

Others felt that the experience of prison did not fulfil its intention as a deterrent measure.

> *You see, what it is, prison don't work. It's the fear of coming to prison that works. And once you're here, it doesn't work... A lot of people are scared to come to prison, but once you're here, it doesn't work. That's why there are a lot of people that re-offend.*
> (Under 18 young man)

Nor did they feel that the severity of the regime necessarily impacted on recidivism[34].

> *I'm not being funny though but I think the harder the prison, the more worse it turns you mentally, you know in your head. The easier it is the more you can deal with it, but the harder it is the stronger it makes you in your head, so you can deal with anything else. So when you do get out you think 'oh prison, I'll do it again'.*
> (Young man)

Those in long-term establishments, doing long sentences, were aware of the influence of bad behaviour on their release dates.

> *There's not much violence in here at all anymore. You hardly see it at all, everyone just wants to get parole, so there's not much fighting.*
> (Young man)

Others were aware that their quality of life was influenced by the ethos and environment of individual establishments. They appreciated the more favourable conditions of the prison they were in compared to those they had already experienced[35].

> *A: Cells are clean*
> *A: Hot radiators*
> *A: The cells are alright, you get your clothes washed*
> *A: You can have a big radio.* (Under 18 young man)

---

34 Rutter, Giller & Hagell (1998) note from their review of the research that custodial care is most likely to be effective if the ethos is prosocial and positive experiences are offered.

35 The importance of a decent physical environment is noted in the monograph 'Psychological Effects of the Prison Environment' (Crabbe, 1997).

The good thing about [open] prison, in bang-up when you get mail sent they open it and read it - in open prison they don't - they just open it in front of your face and leave it, unless there's money put in and they'll take it out. So that's a good thing - you can have your privacy.   *(Young man)*

Many young people expressed exasperation at what they perceived as the illogical implementation of certain establishment regimes and regulations. The incentive scheme was commented upon.

A: *Good's bad.*
A: *There's poor, fair, good, very good and excellent yeah. You've got to get like very good and excellent to keep your points up. If you get good, it's like saying you're average, nothing special, it's not good, not bad. Actually, they're saying it's bad but it will pass.*   *(Young men)*

They say that the main target is to get on enhanced but they try and blackmail you, like 'if you do anything wrong, we'll take you off your enhanced' - and after a while you're not bothered about getting it or not.   *(Young man)*

Young Men and Long-Term Sentences

They've [family] noticed a big difference in me, when I came in I was all 'I've just done this'. I'd got 9 years, I thought I was big - that's not big is it? It's a load of crap man. I thought I might as well sort it out innit? I grew up basically.

That's what you do, you grow up a lot, and you think to yourself 'bloody hell, what am I doing here?'. I've got a younger brother and he's completely different to what I am, completely different, if you'd see my little brother - he goes to college and he does the things that I would like to do when I was his age, but I assumed I was too grown up for my age, I always wanted things that I couldn't have, like driving a car when you're 14, things like that ...

So what's been different, why has he taken that route?

The good part of it is he's seen me and where I've gone wrong and he's thought 'right'. At first he was going down that same road, and then I come to prison, first sentence, and he was still doing the same thing, and I come out and I thought robbery weren't the one and then I started selling drugs, and then I got $3\frac{1}{2}$ for selling drugs and I thought 'well it ain't about that' and then he started college and things like that when I were out. He's only a couple of years younger *than me and I just switched round and got into other things, and things went pear-shaped. But he's thought to himself 'right', he's not doing what I'm doing, he's doing his own thing and he's good man ...*

Has anybody got girlfriends or partners that have stayed with them?

... I said to my girlfriend 'It's not worth it, I'm doing HMP'. So there's no way she's not going to be out there and not get involved in anybody else, she might as well do her own thing.

Not fair on them is it? Making them wait?

It ain't fair on the girl neither is it? Putting her Saturdays aside just for me, she's got work and everything to do. Her own life to live you know what I mean?

What gets you to a point where you think 'I don't want this'?

When I first come to prison my little sister was a baby, she wasn't even 1 years old, used to hold her in me arms and she used to go to sleep and that, I used to love it. And now I speak to her on the phone, like last night I spoke to her on the phone, telling me how she's got her ears pierced, this and that. Mum says she now gets her hair fixed back. I go back to my cell and I think I'm missing all that because of that stupid thing - I'm never coming back to prison. I want to get out and not come to this prison for my little sister and my family, missing them.

Yeah it's about my kid and that, I just want to get out. When I came to prison she weren't even born yet, and now she's 2 nearly 3.

(Young men)

Frustration was expressed in relation to specific regulations such as those relating to the restrictions on items being handed in and the difficulties of having to order goods from outside the establishment.

It's not like they change the rules -it's that they've got different rules for different people. Like ...at Reception you're not allowed big cards, and I got a big card and I weren't allowed a big card, and there's more people I've seen in this jail that's got big cards. They've got rules for different people.   *(Under 18 young woman)*

You have to buy from catalogues so it costs you even more, so like £50 trainers are £80 in the catalogue, it's a rip off. The trainers in there are shit, it's a shit selection as well.   *(Young man)*

Young people made broad recommendations for changing prison rules, proposing that prisoners of all ages should be subject to the same codes of discipline.

> *Q:* *Do you think young people should get better treatment?*
> *A:* *No, one rule for all, it should all be the same. (Young man)*

Others suggested that a more appropriate separation according to age should be considered.

> *A:* *When you're in with older people you feel like you're on another level. Leave the child behind...*
> *A:* *You feel mature man...*
> *A:* *Like when you're in secure, you've got all these little kids in, and you play school rules with them.* (Young men)

Racial Awareness: 'Doesn't this piss you off though – how can the race relations officer be white?'

Young people talked more about issues of cultural stereotyping and racial discrimination when they were discussing aspects of their lives outside prison. But this remark 'how can the race relations officer be white?', voiced by a young black prisoner made a salient point with regard to the cultural background of prison staff. It was hard to take the race relations policy seriously in her view.

Even though comments were infrequent, a significant number of young black people said that they had experienced racism from staff in prison.

Young Women and Racism

Black people in this country, when I got sentenced with my daughter's dad, he's white, an Irish guy, and my step-brother he's white. They done the burglary yeah, and I got done for keeping dog yeah. Now what hurt me the most yeah, when I was in that dock yeah, the judge turned round and blamed me, saying 'it's your fault, if it wasn't for you then these 2 wouldn't have done this crime'. Every time I'm sentenced with a white person I would cop the fucking worst mate, all the time.

It's like when I got nicked in here, 3 of us got nicked ... them 2 got a fine, I got 3 days behind my door. Them 2 are white, I'm half caste.

One, the governor in [name of prison] Mr [name], called me a nigger in adjudication, and I said If I'm a nigger you're a white cunt and I shouldn't have said it, but he called me a nigger.

> *But officers in here... there are no black officers, there's none.*
>
> *Yeah I'm supposed to talk to you about my problems, you know where I'm coming from. Because they think, they're so quick, everything goes wrong because I'm black ...*
>
> *...us two are seen to be the instigators on our wing, because we're black and we're loud, if anything goes wrong on our wing... like the other day the wing kicked off, I went into my room a second time, I thought I ain't got nothing to do with it. I was really proud of myself, you know what I mean. The next day the governor's calling me in the office, so I went in the office, I went 'what' 'I heard that you and [name] were instigating yesterday'. I goes 'check your papers, I was the first one to go back in my cell'. She checked it up yeah, she felt like a right cunt, she had to sit there and apologise to me*
>
> *Even the white inmates can recognise it.*
>
> *...I'm the sort of person right, I'll say it in front of everyone, if I don't have black people around me I start getting withdrawal symptoms, because I just need them around me. When I first got to this jail I thought it's in [county], not far from [city], black people. It's not the case on my landing. When there is too much black people on the landing they start shipping them out. When it gets to 10 people on the landing what do they do?* (Young women)

Bullying in prison: 'Sort it out yourself'

Quite some time was spent talking about bullying and the strategies that could be employed in order to combat it. Everyone agreed that there is bullying in prison. There were however differing views as to how it was handled and what could be done about it.

Sometimes people said that it was known about by staff but that little was done about it.

> *I mean I've seen people getting bullied, I don't think nothing happens...I've seen people get bullied bad and nothing happens about it, when the screws blatantly know about it. (Young woman)*

Others felt that there was more to bullying than thinking it just involved prisoners.

> *It's the screws that are bullying you, that's what I think. It's them screws, prison's all right, it's them screws.* (Young man)

Often people – both young men and young women – felt that it was better to do nothing or 'sort it out yourself' rather than inform staff.

> Q: *So if you thought someone was being bullied where would you take that information– what would you do?*
>
> A: *One thing you don't do in prison is grass, because if you end up grassing, you'll get your head kicked in. Not just by the boy that you're accusing.*   (Under 18 young man)

Some young people felt that the prison criteria for bullying behaviour was sometimes misplaced.

> *I got put on Anti-Bullying Scheme yeah, my own flesh and blood – he didn't have no biscuits so he come up to my pad and I gave him a pack of biscuits, as we walked downstairs, an officer pulled him over and put him on ABS...I give my own flesh and blood a pack of biscuits, what's he going to do, bully me? Fucking hell man, the same genes and that.*   (Young man)

> A: *I've never seen no-one get bullied since I've been here*
> A: *You hear squabbles and arguing*
> A: *You get your arguments, your little fights but that's...you've got 48 women living on a wing, you know what I mean – you get that.*   (Under 18 young women)

A number of young prisoners voiced various strategies for combating bullying, linking it to advice on how to survive in prison.

> *Tell them to keep their head down, stay out of trouble*   (Young man)

> A: *You've got to defend yourself in jail*
> A: *You've got to have eyes in the back of your head*
> A: *If you walk away, you're a muppet then aren't you*
>   (Young men)

> *That's what you got to do in prison, just keep yourself to yourself, don't mouth off to no-one.*   (Under 18 young man)

Drugs and mental health: 'This jail just drugs you up'

Conversations about drug-related issues revolved predominately around lifestyles and events prior to coming into prison. But within the prison context, young people talked about their concerns around both legal and illegal drug taking.

Comments regarding illegal drug-taking in prison were either tied to the notion that cannabis had a calming effect in a stressful environment or that people were turning to hard drugs due to the introduction of mandatory drug testing.

> A: *With the MDTs cannabis stays in your system for 30 days, people are taking harder stuff because it stays in your system less...*
>
> A: *In other prisons I've been in...people are taking stuff that's making them more violent, where they were taking hash before, they were calm, they were fine and everything.*
> *(Young men)*

A number of young people had attended drug awareness courses. Many felt that they would have had more credibility if they had been delivered by 'someone who'd been there'.

> *You should be able to talk to someone who has been there and done it...Like these drug people, oh they get me mad they do. They say 'oh, I understand you' but they don't understand...they don't understand the temptation of heroin addicts and all that, they don't understand nowt.* *(Under 18 young woman)*

> *I've done a drugs course here and the woman that runs it was saying 'I've never done a drug in my life, but if you take this drug, this is the feeling it gives you' - and it makes you think 'hold on a minute, you never done a drug, how can you tell me it makes you feel this way'.* *(Young man)*

Both young men and young women expressed concern about the use of prescribed medication. They felt that to show that they were having difficulties coping or adapting to life in prison increased the chances that they would be administered drugs. This was seldom seen as desirable and a number of young people expressed the view that over-prescribing was commonplace.

> A: *Sleepers or downers, anti-depressants, that'd just fuck your head up even more.*
> Q: *Is that what you'd get if you told people you felt bad?*
> A: *Yeah, you do, you'd get referred to the hospital and if you told them, they'd give you tablets or whatever*
> A: *Yeah, you might even get put over the hospital wing, it depends on how serious it is... best not getting emotional...*
> A: *To be honest with you, I don't care if I'm half-dying, I don't take no drugs, never. I'd rather sweat it out in my cell...*
> A: *If you go down and say you're depressed, they just send you away with drugs, simple, and just send you on your way.*
> *(Young men)*

Any time I come into prison, I am a very hyperactive person, I am loud and bubbly and because I'm loud and bubbly they think I'm doolally. Today they've got me on so much medication yeah and I know it's fucking me up because when I talk I get lockjaw and I sit there sometimes, you know, proper 'dub' and all that ...and like they say to me 'you're on this medication because you need it' and I say 'No I don't need medication, all I need is someone to sit down and talk to, ask me why I'm coming in' (Young woman)

A number of young people had sought alternatives to the medication they were being prescribed for emotional or behavioural problems. They felt that they would prefer to talk to someone about their personal issues. Few said that they found this option open to them.

When I first got sentenced and that I was really fucked up and mad, I was thinking about killing myself and everything, but they didn't want to know nothing about that, they didn't care. I've been on meds. now- how long? I keep putting in an app., everytime I put in an app. to see the psychiatrist they increase my dose I'm like 'No, I want to talk' but it's 'Is anything wrong with your medication?', that's all they care about. (Young woman)

There were few references to suicide attempts or self-harm within the groups, though they were seen as common, especially by the young women. Where mention was made it was mostly to say that they are actions to gain attention, but that this was justified by their past, and current, difficulties.

...I'm not saying that in a bad way, but it is a cry for attention, they're actually saying 'help me here'. I know we all go on when they cut up, and I'm the first to say 'why are you doing it?', but it is a cry for help and they don't get it, staff don't care. (Young woman)

Only one young woman talked about her own self-harm:

It's prison right, when I first got here I thought 'oh yeah, it's laid back, it's all right', I got me head down, I were getting on with it and then I says to them 'I feel like cutting up' they did nothing to help me, I went to me room I got a glass jar, I cut up. The day after I got nicked for having the glass. (Young woman)

Young Men and Hanging

Well I can understand people hanging themselves, but when people cut their wrists that's just nasty, it was just coming out of his arm...When I was in [name of YOI] about three people tried hanging themselves

Everyone used to be at their doors laughing

But it ain't funny, they're mad

If you see for yourself mate, you get a shock

When you hang yourself all problems are solved

No problems are solved, you bring problems to others.
If you're doing a long time, like you get 15 or something then yeah.

Some people hang themselves because they're claustrophobic.

... but when you hang yourself, I reckon at that point when you're choking and there's no air, you want to get your breath back, that's when you change your mind and it's too late.

Every person that I've known that's hanged themselves, they've pushed the bell, before they hanged themselves. What's the point of that if you're going to hang yourself, you don't push the bell so the governor comes up and stops you killing yourself do you?

If you want to hang yourself, you could ask me, I'll make you a noose yeah, emergency release in it.

(Under 18 young men)

The young people did give examples of prison environments that had been supportive and given them an opportunity to tackle personal issues. Having someone who listened was key.

A: *[name of prison] is the best prison I've ever been to. When I were in that prison I felt like a new person.*

Q: *What was it that made it good?*

A: *It ain't even the houses, forget that, that it isn't a bang up, (...) I was a bitch a proper cold hearted bitch, I was a bully, I was going round intimidating people. The governor called me into his office, sat me down, he goes 'look [name], forget that I'm the governor, what is your problem, how can I help you?' You know what I mean? They got me on counselling, I didn't have no medication, anger management course, relaxation two times a week. It was really good...*   *(Young woman)*

Relationships with other prisoners: 'I wouldn't trust no-one'

Many of the young people were ambivalent about their relationships with other prisoners. They saw that they needed to retain an element of independence.

> A: *I come in on me own, I go home on me own. You make good friends but you've never got a best friend...*
> A: *I wouldn't really trust anybody...*
> A: *Yeah, it's true. You've got to be wary, even though you watch each other, you've still got to watch your own back and what you're saying.*   (Young women)

Even though most people agreed that they would 'look out for each other' the predominant view was that each person ultimately had to do their own time.

> *I wouldn't trust no-one. I make mates but I never make a friend.*
>   (Young man)

Among young men in prison, it was apparent that attitudes towards sex offenders often reflect the attitudes of intolerance voiced by men in the adult system.

> *...walking round blatant all over the wings, and when we're in for normal crimes and you're thinking 'bloody hell, he's raped a woman, that could've been my little girl' – it sends your head, it makes you feel sick.*   (Young man)

Young people did, however, seek to maintain strong ties with their friends and families outside the prison.

Maintaining contact with outside: 'I don't know how my mum found it'

Young people had a strong sense of the strain placed on families in order to maintain contact.

> A: *You know what? I'm not bothered about myself, I'm bothered about my family. You know what I mean? I aren't bothered about myself...*
> A: *It's not just you that's going through it, is it? It's your mam and dad, your brothers and sisters and all that.*
>   (Under 18 young woman)

The vast majority of young people maintained relationships with at least one parent. These were kept going through visits which were limited more by geographical location rather than any reluctance on the part of the visitors [36]

When I was at [name of establishment], it was 10 minutes away, took my mum 10 minutes. To get here takes 2¹/₂ hours.

(Young woman)

I've been in this jail for 8 month without a visit. I want to go to another jail that's closer to home so I can get my visits.

(Young man)

The first visit, the Saturday after I came, I don't know how my mum found it, it's kind of like far away though for a visit.

(Under 18 young man)

For some families, it all proves too much.

I haven't had any visits or phone-calls.   *(Young woman)*

It's too far for my mam to come down.

(Under 18 young woman)

For some young women, there is the added stress of managing their relationship with their own children.

My co-accused – she's just had a baby – she asks the governor, puts in for home leave – she wants to take the baby home to get it used to things. You know what they said? They can hand it out on a weekend. Now, that's bang out of order that...'You can hand it out to your mum and dad or the baby's father'. That is bang out of order that.   *(Under 18 young woman)*

Even though links to the outside were often tenuous and difficult to maintain, they were valued highly by most of the young people.

---

36   In reviewing secure treatment outcomes Bullock et al. (1998) noted that more could be done to draw relatives into the treatment process and to link institutional and community intervention.

4 Preparation and Planning for Life Outside Prison

Young people gave the impression that they had used a considerable amount of time in prison to consider their hopes, fears and prospects for life outside. They often talked aspirationally about their future lives but were acutely aware that outside society was not necessarily going to be easy to adapt to.

To draw out young people's opinions about how life outside would be the conversations were guided towards thinking about how prison prepares them for release; if they thought they would be able to stay away from re-offending; possible ways to prevent young people from offending; whether they had plans for housing and employment and the barriers to these; and, in turn, how they could help their own children not to offend.

In the groups the young people talked about how they would survive in what they saw as an uncompromising environment. Their views frequently echoed government concerns around re-offending and prevention of ongoing cycles of criminality.

Concern about the outside world: 'What is this world coming to?'

Many young offenders expressed concerns about aspects of outside life that they felt were linked to their own lives and to the continuation of a young prison population. Many were worried that young children were taking drugs.

> *I read in the paper about an eight year old smack head. What is this world coming to?* (Young woman)

Alcohol was seen by some to be an issue too.

> *They're starting younger. Yeah it's getting worse. You see little 9 year olds outside the off-license going 'Buy me that, go buy me some drink'. 'No mate you're too young'.* (Young man)

Others were concerned about the opening of secure training centres for young children.

> *I can't believe it, they're making a wing for 10 year olds. What's it going to be next? Are they going to start branding people and stuff like that, putting marks on them? Are they going to make a wing for babies, babies going out killing people?* (Young man)

What will it be like out there? 'Everything's just right fast'

A few found thinking about life outside prison simply too distressing.

> *Don't even fucking think about it, if you think about your freedom and getting out and shit like that, your head's just going to end up in bits. If you get your head round your jail before you know it time's flying by.* (Young man)

However, most of the young people spent a considerable amount of time thinking about what their lives would be like outside prison.

> *Well when you're in your cell, I don't know about anyone else but I just lie back and think about life, how it's going to be for me for the rest of my life.* (Young man)

Alongside thoughts of the future, family, jobs, home, there were some anxieties and fears.

> *When you haven't been out for a while everything's just right fast, because you're doing all the same thing all the time in here, but when you get out everything's right fast, cars flying by you and everything, it's mad.* (Young man)

> *Like you get one town visit and then you're out, bam, you're on the road and you've been outside of society for years and then, bam, you're back. It's like, even in your own town, you're in a time warp. Everything's changed.* (Young man)

A number of young people referred to ways in which they could make a less sudden entry into the outside world.

> *For your last three months or summat, getting released once a week for a day, just to wean your way out of the system gradually. Instead of straight back into it, everything's at 100 miles an hour.*
> (Young man)

In one particular focus group the young men talked about their dependence on prison and the problems associated with leaving.

A: *Young men get institutionalised as well Miss, because you're young Miss, you don't know that much about the outside world because you're always in and out of jail, so it comes to a point where all you really know about is jail, you get me? It's the only place you feel safe and secure.*

A: *Some people can't hack it when they're outside. They need a stable environment. They need jail. Like jail keeps some people alive. Look at all the drug addicts that keep coming to jail, if they hadn't have had those spells in jail, they'd be dead now wouldn't they? You know jails kept some of them alive.*

A: *I feel pissed off when I come into jail, I also feel pissed off when I get out, like I can't win.*   (Young men)

Some young people anticipated the kind of negative reception they were likely to get back in the community.

My mum was saying... she can't even go to the shops now because people are coming up to her saying 'Ah your son's in prison'...... But it's hard because I know when I go back it's going to be hard to mix in that atmosphere, because people look at you in a criminal way, just give you dirty looks and things like that.
                              (Under 18 young man)

A group of young women talked about this issue.

A: *'I've been to jail, I'm a big girl', if I walked out and said that, my dad'd just backhand me right away.*

A: *That's why I'm ashamed of going back out.*

A: *My dad doesn't even tell his brothers or his sisters I'm in jail.*

A: *I've ashamed my family.*

A: *When I go back to town, you know what it's like where I live, when I go back to our town it'll be like 'she's just got out' and they'll all be round.*   (Young women)

Preparing for release: 'I felt like a lost sheep when I got out'

While imprisoned, many young people thought a great deal about their own forthcoming release and were concerned about the way in which others were discharged summarily from their sentences.

He was on anti-depressants, forever cutting up, needed attention all the time. Four o'clock in the afternoon the screws come round 'pack your kit, you're going home'. I felt dead sorry for her, she had no-where to go,

no mum or no dad, dumped outside the gates, knowing full well that she's got nowhere to go, and like basically 'do your own thing'.
(Young woman)

There's people in here now that have got nowhere to live and that. What are they going to do? Come the day they get out with their £35 and they kick them out, say 'see you in a couple of weeks'.
(Young man)

They talked about their own previous experience of leaving prison.

I felt like a lost sheep when I got out. I didn't know whether to go this way or that, me head were in bits, I didn't know what to do. I thought where can I go, what can I do.　　　　*(Young man)*

They were aware not only of what they hoped for themselves but of the expectations of other people in their lives outside prison.

You see, my ex-boyfriend died of a drug overdose and people say to me 'because he's died, why don't you change your life?'. But I'm trying to say to people I want to change my life, but I'm scared, I don't know where to start, what to do.　　　　*(Young woman)*

Some young people had been helped to prepare for release, in particular by gaining vocational skills and qualifications, by coming off drugs and by being enabled to stop and think. But most young people thought that they were not prepared at all for life outside prison.

Q:　What goes on in preparing you for getting out?
A:　Nothing. You get released, you sign your discharge grant, you sign your travel warrant and that's it, see you later.
(Young man)

Probability of re-offending: 'It's the same circle over and over again'

Very few young people planned to continue offending following their release from prison but almost all acknowledged the difficulty they would experience trying to stay out of trouble[37] .

I'm getting out in 12 weeks and I'm getting so scared, because it's easy to say 'I'm not going to get into trouble' but it really creeps on me, like trouble just finds me.　　　　*(Young woman)*

37　The Howard League Report 'Sentenced to Fail' (Grindrod, 1998) sees substantial through-care and after-care as essential to prevent re-offending.

Despite good intentions it would be all too easy to resume a familiar lifestyle.

I can imagine you get back there and you get banged into the system again and you think 'ah jail, that's in the past' and then you're back into your old ways again, and before you know it you're back in jail thinking 'I wish I'd never done that'. But shit happens though doesn't it? (Young man)

You're just going to get back to the way it was before aren't you? Because I know I am. But in here I can say 'Oh I'm not going to do this, I'm not going to do that' but when I get out I'm going to do it all again. (Young woman)

The primary reasons for re-offending were seen as the return to high crime estates, no jobs, peer pressure, the temptation of drugs and drink, survival and the need for money.

A lot of it's boredom, if you've got nothing to do, if you're sat at home twiddling your thumbs. What can I do. I haven't got a job. I know I'll go and rob a car. I'll go and see me mates. I need some money, go and get some drugs, so I'll go and rob this, rob that, before you know it you're back in here. (Young man)

Drugs and drink: 'Look I'm turning back into a junkie, help me.'

Many young people believed that a return to drug taking and/or heavy drinking would be the most likely precipitating factors leading to re-offending.

I'm a smackhead. I've been a smackhead from the age of 13. It's the same cycle over. And when I get out I know exactly what I'm going to do. Go out back on drugs. It's the only life I know and it's crime. (Young woman)

If someone's an addict, yeah 99 per cent they're going to come back, because they're just going into the same lifestyle. (Young woman)

A number of young people spoke of their determination to stay off drugs. Most believed that to do so they would need substantial support and after-care from people who really understood about drug taking.

Like these drug people, oh they get me mad, they do. They say 'Oh, I understand you'. but they don't understand. They ask you why you keep going out. They don't understand the temptation of heroin addicts, and all that, they don't understand nowt. They just think that you can come to jail, stop your drugs, go out and you're alright, but it doesn't work like that. It's temptation, not withdrawal, it's temptation nowt else. (Young woman)

It was noticeable that young women talked more than the young men in groups about the need to kick a drink or drugs habit.

Young Women and Drugs

If I go home and have a dig of smack I will probably OD because the amount I used to take and I'd go out and I'd think 'that's nowhere near the amount I used to have' and I'd just put a bit on the spoon, but I know I'd OD, and honestly [name] you wanted to see me, I was a proper mess, I were proper skinny but I thought that I looked nice like, proper black round me eyes. I have no enamel on me teeth at the back through putting smack and coke on me teeth. Marks on me arms, I've got scars. I'll try not to, I can say I won't have a dig, I will not have a dig, I don't want marks on me arms, I've got them in places... you can't really see where I've injected, but I can't handle it, I couldn't cope with it. I think I were going fucking mad me before, I really do. I just didn't give a fuck anymore.

When you're a smackhead, it's the same thing you go out, you rob, you graft, you sell your stuff, you score, you're mongy when you get up, you do the same every single day. Nothing occurs in your head, nothing just that.

A dig in the morning, have a goutch, come out of goutch, me and me brother will wake up, say 'come on let's go out grafting', do the graft, score, go down Asda, get me Mr Kipling's apple pies and custard, doughnuts, come back home, have something to eat, have a dig. And that's all I did.

You don't really meet anybody else apart from....

Unless they come up to me and go '[name] do you want to score' and I'd go like that, that'd be the only way I'd talk to someone, if it were owt to do with smack, can I rip them off by £50, that's the only time I'd talk to anyone.

I'm shitting myself about going home, shitting it. I'm going out to me brother, and me probation say 'you can't see your brother [name], you can't go around with your brother'. He's me fucking brother, my brother brought me up more than me mum. I can't fuck me brother off after all he's done for me, he needs help, and I'm going to go back to him.

Yeah but is he going to drag you down though?

> *That's what I'm saying, I don't know. He doesn't want me to go back on heroin, he's me fucking brother, he cares about me. But getting out there to see all that shit again, it'll proper freak me out... The only thing that'll be different now is that I'll go 'come on [name] I'm going to try and do me rattle' and he'll be like 'go on then' and he'd always give up before me. I'd come down in the morning, you know how you come down with the quilt round you sit down and that, and he'd be cooking up, how'm I meant to do a rattle if someone's cooking up in front of me. But this time I can go out and I'm actually off gear, and I can get up without having back ache and spewing up and fucking falling on floor because I'm too weak to walk, and I can go out and I can be 'fucking hell man sort your head out'. This is the only time I'll probably be able to help him any more than I have been able to before.* (Young women)

Drink was often used to avoid difficulties and to blank everything out.

> *It's like me with drink, everything gets on top, I just run for the bottle. But the drink just makes it worse because I'm blocking it out, and really you have to be brave and you have to face it, you do. You have to face it. You have to be strong enough.* (Young woman)

> *When I get out I'm not going to drink as much as I used to. I used to drink lager at 9 o'clock in the day. Get up, have a lager, and I've got me baby there and I never once thought 'baby'. Well I did, but I used to drink only lager and I'd leave the baby in bed .....and I wouldn't go to bed until it had all gone.* (Young woman)

Drugs and drink were seen to be part of a vicious circle. While drugs were seen as likely to lead to robbing or stealing to feed the habit, drink was seen as likely to lead to fights and assaults.

> A: *Yeah, if you've had a drink all night, and someone just walks past you and they could just bump you by accident, you can turn round and it just kicks off and that.*
> A: *The first thing you do when you get out is to go out and get bladdered isn't it?* (Young men)

The lack of preparation for release was much criticised. Most young people thought that support and after-care were an important safety net after custody. They needed someone to turn to if they were to resist a return to drink or drugs.

> *No they need to do a lot more with after-care. All right you can throw people in prison and say you've got to stop doing it, but where's the help to stop doing it? Throwing you back out to society, what do they*

do then? They've got no job, no money, so they're going to turn to drugs, what can you expect? (*Young woman*)

A number of young women who had used drugs wanted advice and support which went beyond just getting clean needles. They wanted help to stop and think, to weigh up pros and cons and to stay clean.

A: *I've reached that stage, I don't want to go out back on gear.*

A: *I have not got that endurance you know, I cannot say what its like because I don't know. I don't know what its like.*

A: *Well look at me, perfect example – I lasted 4 weeks outside, and to me something's wrong, and if the Government can't see that.*

Q: *So you're saying more support outside?*

A: *Definitely. What I done yeah when I got out for those 4 weeks I went to my probation officer. I cried my eyes out and said 'look I'm turning back into a junkie, help me' and she just sat there, give me a tissue and said 'there's a drugline in town centre, go there'. And I thought if she can't help me...* (*Young women*)

You come out and your mates round here are smoking crack or smoking heroin and its making you think 'right give us some of that'. As soon as you smoke that's, it's the same thing, back to square one and it doesn't help. But if you have someone trying to show you what the bad points are and what you're doing to your family and this and that, I think you've got more chance to say to yourself, to think back and say 'if I smoke some of that is it worth it? This is going to happen and that is going to happen.' And you don't really need all of that, you know what I'm saying? (*Young man*)

Peer pressure: 'It's the wrong crowd I'm mixing up with'

A number of young people were aware that they needed to steer clear of some old friends' on release if they were to avoid re-offending.

That's why I'm moving me, because it's the wrong crowd I'm mixing up with. (*Young woman*)

I mean I've done crimes, come to jail, come out done about a week. I don't want to get in with the same crowd again. But then like a week later, I'm like 'Oh, I don't care'. Start going a bit mental again. (*Young man*)

For some it wasn't so much the case of direct influence by peers but rather a need to re-establish a reputation within the peer group that was likely to lead to re-offending[38] .

Then you go to the prison and that's it you're out of their lives, and someone else is there, taking your place, making the money, driving the flashy cars or whatever. Then you get out and nobody knows you, so you're nobody no more and you think 'I want to get that back'. So you go out there and do all those dodgy things that you shouldn't be doing to get back up there again.   (Young man)

Getting into fights with other young people was seen as a likely route back into prison. Most believed that it would be difficult to walk away from an incident. They would have to defend themselves, regardless of the consequences.

I'm not going to go out and do another street robbery. I'm not going to go out robbing. I'm not going to do owt to come back to prison, but I can't say I won't go out one night and a lass could start on me, and smack me, I smack her back. We get caught and I could come to prison for it.   (Under 18 young woman)

The prospect of re-offending loomed large for many young people. A number believed that you can 'never say never' when it comes to going back to prison. Most were aware of high levels of re-offending and the probability of being sent down again.

It ain't rehabilitation, because you come in here and see people that have been in 3 or 4 times.   (Young man)

But in all the groups, young people still talked a lot about their hopes and plans for the future.

They had clear ideas about what might stop them getting into trouble again. These included being a parent; housing; qualifications and employment; having someone to turn to; stopping and thinking; staying off drink and drugs; and, lastly, self determination, 'it's down to me'.

Being a parent: 'Maybe they can learn from my mistakes'

There were young parents in all of the groups. They and other young men and women responded seriously to questions about their actual or future roles and responsibilities as parents. Many believed that they could make a

---

38   Emler & Reicher (1995) address the issue of reputation management and the importance of adhering to the group position on delinquency to ensure acceptance in the group.

better job of parenting than their own parents had. They placed a strong emphasis on talking to, and understanding their children.

I want to be able to understand my son, because my mum isn't an understanding person, she's very old fashioned in her ways. She's a modern mum, she's only 38, but she never used to talk about sex and she's wondering why I'm pregnant at 15, she never sat me down and told me about the birds and the bees. (Under 18 young woman)

I'd just talk to them instead of punish them, maybe they can learn from my mistakes. Like my dad was an ex-army man, so I could never talk to him, he was proper strict. He didn't like me. I didn't like him. In the start he did, he tried to, but when I got older he didn't like me. So try and talk to them, just be their mate and don't punish them. (Young man)

Ask them their problems, know what's going on, you know what I mean, and do my best to help it. Because I know I never got it. I never got asked what was wrong with me, I just got slapped. I had everything when I was younger, but I never had love. But my child, I know if I've turned out badly I know one thing good's going to come out of it - my child won't turn out badly. (Young woman)

The majority believed that they could keep their children out of trouble and saw this as an important goal. This was a strongly held view despite a recurring theme in groups that the young people's own parents could try as hard as they liked but they were powerless to intervene to prevent offending. Strategies included:

You have to give them 100 per cent attention. (Under 18 young man)

Make sure they don't hang around with the wrong crowd and that, send them to good school, make them do their homework, bring them up right. (Under 18 young man)

Give them things, if they've achieved staying out of trouble for two weeks, so like you know ....do something with them, something they'd enjoy. Make them respect you. (Young man)

My mum wasn't there to tell me, she wasn't there, I was in care. When you're young in care at that age, you don't have no one telling you 'you can't have stuff'. You do your own thing. At the end of the day, I want to be my daughter's friend, but I ain't going to be soft, you've got to put your foot down as well. Over my dead body is my daughter going to be 13 taking drugs, doing everything what I was doing. Even if she hates me, I don't care because I know she'll look back and say 'Thanks mum'. (Young woman)

Many young parents were critically aware that they, or their families, were poor role models for their children.

Q: *If you've got kids of your own, how do you actually stop them? Can you stop them?*

A: *Bring them up the right way, don't do what you done.... If you ain't got a job, say a kid asks his dad 'what job have you got?' and he says 'ah, I'm a robber'. Yeah he's a robber, I'm going to be a robber as well innit....*

A: *My dad was never around, I have to go and visit him in Majorca if I wanted, to see him once a year. I wouldn't want to mix with him anyway. Not the right people. People that shoot people and stuff.*

A: *If your dad's got a job and he goes to work every day, that's what his kid's going to want to do isn't it?*

A: *They follow the family footprints innit.*   **(Young men)**

Some of the young people felt strongly that they needed to try and bring up their own children in a different environment away from negative influences.

Q: *But do you want to bring your kids up the way you were brought up?*

A: *I was on about leaving today, because at the end of the day all my family's smackheads, all my son comes in contact with. Before he grows up and he says 'me dad's a smackhead, me uncle's a smackhead, me cousin's a smackhead, me mum's friend's a smackhead, so it's alright to take it.' How can I sit my son down and say 'don't take it' when he sees his dad taking it? I've got to get away, I need to.*   **(Young woman)**

One or two young people felt strongly that they would hate their child to know that they had spent time in prison.

I wouldn't want my kid to find out I'd come to prison, I'd be devastated.   **(Young man)**

Most thought that they could use their experience of prison as a deterrent for their own child.

Well I can tell him what it's like inside. I've just finished a parentcraft course so I've got a bit more things to tell him.[39]
   (Young man)

---

[39]   TSA is currently conducting a 2 stage evaluation of parenting courses for Young Offenders, which follows them on release from custody. The results of this project will be available in February 2000.

I can't stop him doing bad things, I can't stop him because I'm not going to be with him 24 hours a day. But when he gets older I'll tell him what prison's like. I can't really tell him what you'll feel like because I won't know what he'll feel like but I can tell him what I felt like at that time, stupid... (Young man)

I'm going to say 'look at me, this is what I've done, this is the mistakes I've made. What do you want to do in life? Do you want to turn out like me or do you want to sort your life out and that?' (Young woman)

A number of young parents talked about how much they missed their own children. Many believed, or hoped, that on release from prison they would do things differently and 'be there' for their children. For some, being a parent was seen as the primary reason for not re-offending[40].

It's made me wake up and that, I've got a kid and that on the out, a 4 year old son and when I were messing about I didn't see him, didn't realise how much he meant, and now I'm in here, that's an incentive for me not to come back. I'm not going to come that, but you can't say that – I'm going to do me best not to come back. (Young man)

Quite a few young offenders saw their relationship with their own family, not necessarily their own child, as central to staying out of custody. Some believed that feelings about their attachments to their own parents would keep them out of jail. Family ties and support, or lack of them, were seen to matter very much.

I've put my mum through too much to come back here. (Under 18 young woman)

I wouldn't do it again because I've been away from me family, but if I didn't have no family or nowt, then I wouldn't think twice about doing a crime and coming back here. (Under 18 young woman)

Somewhere to live and enough to live on: 'Enough money to get you on your feet'

Young people saw housing and money as fundamental to staying out of crime. One or two were keen to point out that they were only seeking a very basic level of support on release from custody.

---

41   Lloyd (1995) documents the negative impact of imprisonment on the children of prisoners.

I don't want to live off the state, I just want some support, that's it.
(Young woman)

The lack of benefits for the under 18s was keenly felt.

A: *I'm not even going to have no money when I go out.*

A: *I won't get nothing then.*

A: *How old are you?*

A: *17*

A: *You won't get nothing.*

A: *She's old enough to get a job but she's not old enough to get some money when she's out. That's stupid. You're old enough to get married but....*

A: *At the end of jail right when you've come out of jail and you've not got enough money to support you, that's why you commit offences like that isn't it, do you know what I mean?*
(Young women)

I tell you what it is right, after you get out, on to probation the other day: 'Discharge', he says 'you'll get money the first week but on the second week you'll have no money, how do you think about that?' And I looked at him and said 'I'm very lucky that I'm with me mum, but what if I wasn't with me mum, living in a hostel and only enough money for one week, what you gonna do for the next week?'
(Young woman)

There were those who were going out to face debts and financial difficulties.

I owe loads of money   *(Under 18 young woman)*

A: *When you go to Social Security, they'll say 'You've got £37 off the prison, come back next week'.*

A: *Do they realise how much money's needed to live out there? They don't.*

A: *It's £3.50 for a packet of ciggies.*

A.   *Nappies and baby wipes, £10: £7 in Pampers and £3 in baby wipes.*
(Young women)

Some young people were counting on support from family or friends.

My family is saving up money for me now, putting money away for the last 3 years, and they've give it to me and I'm going to start up – that's why I'm doing this course – I'm going to start my own business up.
(Young man)

I know when I get out there, well before I get out hopefully, I'm going to get a house. I'm going to settle in and me boyfriend's going to get out of jail and I'm just going to live with him. (Young woman)

Help with housing and resettlement was seen as a priority, particularly by the young women.

But all they ask you is 'Where did you live before, have you got anywhere to go to?' that's it, see you later. What they should do with sentence planning, they can't guarantee that everyone's going to go out and get somewhere but they should try, they should get on to your probation officer, even if they just put in a referral.
(Young woman)

A number of young people thought that there should be more hostels. Ideally they should be protective environments.

And more hostels, because the main thing is drugs and homelessness, that's what's the matter at the end of the day.
(Young woman)

Many young people were very critical of current hostel provision.

Q: Do they help you with things like housing?
A: They'd just send you to a dosshole full of smackheads and that, and you'd end up back on it. That's what they did to me anyway.
Q: Is that the hostels?
A: Yeah. Full of people injecting smack and that, so I were coming out of prison and going into another prison, really.
(Young man)

Something to do: 'If you're interested in something you stick to it'

While getting a job or continuing with education were seen as primary goals, many young people thought that, if these were not possible, it was still important to have something to keep them occupied. An interest or a sense of direction were considered important.

If you get them interested in something, if you're interested in something you stick at it...You tend to realise where you're going... If you like football or something like that, it doesn't matter if you're not really good at it. (Under 18 young man)

Some felt that hanging around on the streets with nothing to do could lead to getting involved in crime again. A few young people thought that having an activity or interest could be a counterweight to this.

Things that you enjoy, get your adrenaline going. You can get things that are legal that can do that, you get some courses, like bikes and things like that, things that young guys are into and that, that'll help you know what I mean? And it's no good just having them in jail, you need something to fall back on when you get out of jail as wall, even if it's just twice a week, that's twice a week off the streets innit? You know what I mean when you get out? (Young man)

Education and employment: 'It's harder getting a job when you've been in prison'

Most of the young people believed that getting a job was critical to settling down after prison. Many thought that this would be very difficult after a sentence. The need for more help ranging from vocational training, to work preparation and job seeking was a recurring theme.

I think good counselling, you know, to get you a job so that you don't just get kicked out of the gates with £35 in your hand, nowhere to go. At least you've got a job to go out to haven't you?

(Young man)

A significant minority of the young people had been successful in developing vocational skills and gaining qualifications in prison. They believed that this would stand them in good stead.

A: *I've got me appointment on Tuesday if I get me home leave. I've been doing hairdressing here and I've done me level 1 and I'm starting level 2, so I'm going to go to college and carry on with that.*

Q. *So that sounds as if prison's been a bit useful for you?*

A. *Yeah it has, education. I've got my health and social care, I've just passed 3 of the exams.* (Young woman)

I've done a painting and decorating course, and now I'm doing a bricklaying course - which I learn to build walls and houses. If I do that and I go to a building site, they're not going to say 'where've you been?'. If I can do that, if I'm good at bricklaying, I can say 'any chance of a job?' and do bricklaying for a bit. It's a job isn't it, as soon as you're out there. (Young man)

While employment or further education was a key priority for nearly all the young men, there were marked differences between those who believed that they had a chance of gaining work and others who thought that, with a criminal record, there was no probability of being offered work in the first place, or of being trusted by an employer.

Those who did feel that they could get work knew that they would need to make an extra effort to prove themselves and that they would need to find an employer prepared to give them a chance.

> A: *I like to work, yeah. If I've got a job, I'll do it. It's pointless being there if you're not going to do it, that's how I look at it. So if I went out there and got a job on a building site, and they said 'Right you've been in jail, I'm not going to look at that. I'm going to look at the way you work first. I'm going to give you a two week trial, because I don't think that going to make much difference. If you can work, you can work, simple as that.' So they give you a two week trial. You work your bollocks off, you graft, yeah fair enough. Doesn't matter if you've been in jail, if you graft hard they'll give you a job. That's how I think it should be anyway.*
>
> A: *Yeah I'm working on wood skills now and doing an NVQ in carpentry, so when I've done that I can be a carpenter. I doubt I'll finish it by the time I get out, but if I'd finished it I'd have a national, recognised qualification wouldn't I? I could take that to a job and say 'well I've got that'.*
>
> Q: *Do you think that would over-ride being in jail?*
>
> A: *No. People just see jail. It's tunnel vision: jail, bad, criminal, thief, murderers, rapists.*
>
> Q: *But you still do the course?*
>
> A: *I'd still do the course because some people will look at you, might give you a chance. They've got patience, other people haven't.*   (Young men)

The majority of young people believed that having a job was crucial to staying away from crime.

Young Men, Work and their Criminal Record

It's harder getting a job when you've been in prison, you go for some job interviews when you've been in prison ... maybe you'll come across some who won't, but the majority of them when you've been in prison, so you go grafting with your mates and you end up back here. That's what most of the people come back in for, not a lot of people are willing to give you a chance, they're not interested, you've been to prison.

As soon as they hear 'prison' nah, don't want you, or 'we'll get back in contact with you' and you never hear nothing. It's like if you sign up with an agency and are honest with them and say you've got a police record, they say 'oh we might have some work for you' but most places won't take you and you don't hear nothing from them, they don't want to know. So you're in a no-win situation.

I don't think it should matter. I don't think you should have to tell them, unless it's for paedophile or rapist, and obviously you should have to tell them then ... but burglaries and stuff like that, assaults, drugs, I don't think you should have to be honest about it, have to tell them.

Or you should have something like agencies for previous people who'd been in prison, people who've just got out who want a job and that, sign up with an agency for ex-prisoners.

Help you get a job yeah.

You've come to jail for assault, and you go for a job interview, they just automatically think 'oh he's violent, if he loses his rag he's going to get smacked'. It's not like that though is it.

... in a job you're not going to get someone who's going to come up to you and try and whack you really?

(Young men)

No more crime: '...when you decide, yeah. When you get some sense in your head. When you grow up a bit'.

Most of the young people in the focus groups hoped not to re-offend. Many feared they might, and two or three knew they would.

Myself, I'm not going to change until I'm ready to, am I? There's nothing anybody can do for me. There may be a day when I'm sitting in an adult jail in 5 years time, 6 years time, and I'm going to go and say 'enough's enough for me'. But these people talking shite to you while you're in here, it's not for me. (Young man)

One or two others thought they might be deterred by the increased probability of getting caught.

> *Look at the computers, I heard that in the millennium they're going to be broken down. They're going to be fucked, a lot of them. Don't think they're not going to come up with something better this time. They're going to come with something better for the millennium. And they're going to use a computer. A computer can do so much. They can just give it your last name and they know about your life. And then your picture will come up and what crime…You ain't going to want to be doing no more crime. It's done with now. I think people should just try to go the right way now. That's basically what I think anyway.* (Under 18 young man)

The majority were committed to trying to stop offending and to staying out of prison. A central belief emerged that, when it came to it, only the young people themselves could effect change.

> *You've got to want to change it yourself. They can't change you. You've got to want to do it yourself, decide.* (Young man)

> A: *Its up to you at the end of the day. You only stop doing crime if you want to do it inside. Sometimes you may say you want to stop, but inside you don't really want to stop. You only stop when you want to do it inside.*
>
> A: *When you decide it, yeah. When you get some sense in your head. When you grow up a bit.* (Under 18 young men)

Many young people saw being prepared to change as part of becoming more mature. They thought that younger adolescents might not be ready to listen to adults or to change their behaviour:

> *It goes in one ear and out the other innit? That's when you're young and you don't give a fuck!* (Young man)

A number of young people very much regretted that they had spent their teenage years growing up in prison.

> A: *I'm 20 now and since I've been 15 I've been in and out of jail. I've spent the best part of 5 years in jail, and I've made no life for myself. I could have done a lot of things in that time.*
>
> Q: *Do you reckon you still could now?*
>
> A: *Yeah I'm still only young, just 20 now, so I've got a life ahead of me, so its just thinking 'what can I do when I get out?'*
> (Young men)

The majority recognised that young people can, and do, change. Only one or two thought they would stay involved in crime. Most young people thought that they would grow up and stop offending at some time, probably in their twenties[41]. The pressing need for support after prison[42], and someone to talk to, was either explicitly stated or implied by many young people.

---

41 Bullock et al (1998) noted that for young people leaving secure treatment centres to achieve good outcomes, support is needed up to the age of 21, but preferably up to the age of 25.

42 Graham & Bowling (1995) found that 'growing out of crime' is now occurring at a slower rate. Many of the young people in their sample had not completed the transition to adulthood, and away from crime, by their mid 20's.

5 Key Messages from Young People

In these groups young people worked hard to explain their pathways into crime, their experience of prison and their hopes and fears for the future. From the discussions, insights emerged with clear implications for policy and practice. The picture the young men and women presented was complex. They could see no single or easy solutions. In their view immediate change is called for on a number of levels.

The young people were perceptive. Most had clear ideas about how they had become involved in offending and were critically aware of how difficult it would be to avoid re-offending. Their assessment of the causal factors of youth crime, and the ways in which these factors interact, reflect the research evidence. Their ideas about what can be done to reduce youth crime, and what are the potential points for intervention, endorse the Government's agenda for crime reduction and reform of the youth justice system.

What is particular to this focus group research is the voice of young people in custody themselves and their preparedness to consider what needs to be changed. Their insights and views are drawn from memories of everyday life in their own communities and their current dislocated experience of everyday life in prison. Few, if any, would know of the research evidence. It is fair to say that the young people in the groups were not aware of new legislation, policy direction or practice initiatives. Yet they share an awareness of what needs to change and they have some fresh ideas about how to effect change. The Government's commitment to seeing young people as an essential part of the solution, not just as part of the problem is important. Most of the young people appreciated being consulted. This might indicate that other ways could be found to involve them directly in the process of change.

A number of key messages emerged from discussions in the groups. These show stages where it may be possible to break what the young people describe as 'the same circle over and over again'.

Within the community:

- To prevent children and young people becoming involved in crime, design interventions that target the very young.

- Don't blame parents, focus on improving communication between parents and teenagers.

- Clean up the estates and improve poor living conditions, where violence, drug dealing and crime are just part of everyday life.

- Marginalised young people, including those who don't or can't go to school, still want to learn and should be involved in education.

- Disrupted lives can be a route to offending, children and young people in local authority care need continuity and stability. They need someone, or just a few people they can trust and rely on over time.

- Young people are influenced a great deal by their friends, so find ways to make positive uses of peer group pressure.

- To prevent offending, tackle drug and alcohol abuse, in particular, target hard drug dealers and suppliers and take drugs off the streets and out of schools and colleges.

Within the criminal justice system:

- Tackle racism in every area of the criminal justice system and ensure fair, respectful and appropriate treatment for young black people.

- Pay particular attention to improving relations between the police and young people.

- Court processes should be quicker and clearer. Judges and magistrates should be more in touch with young people's lives.

- Sentencing should be fairer, eradicating any gender, race and regional bias. Community sentences must have more credibility and relevance.

- Youth justice and probation workers should be visible, consistent and effective.

In prison

- Staff should treat children and young people with respect. They should be trained to understand that young people are growing up while they are in prison.

- Make prisons safe for young people by tackling bullying, racism and offending behaviour in the institution.

- Prison rules and procedures should be clear and fair if they are to be understood by young people.

- Make proper use of induction, sentence planning and personal officer schemes to guide young people through their time in prison.

- To reduce the risk of re-offending, offending behaviour programmes, education, and preparation for work must all be given priority.

- Tackle the use of illegal drugs in prison.

- Reduce the use of prescribed drugs by improving health care and emotional support for young people.

- Prisons for young people should be much more connected to the outside world: families, carers, friends, youth justice workers.

- Prepare young people properly for release and create opportunities to adjust more gradually to life in the community.

Life after prison

- To reduce the risk of re-offending, young people need after-care and close support following their release from prison.

- Young people need particular help to stay off drugs, preferably from ex-users who know from experience how difficult this process is.

- Provide young people with practical help with housing and resettlement and create drug free hostels.

- 16 to18 year olds leaving prison need adequate benefits or wages to survive in the community.

- Help young people to prepare for, and to get real jobs, possibly by setting up agencies for young ex-offenders.

- Young parents in prison want to be good parents to their own children. They may need support to overcome difficulties in trying to resume their responsibilities.

- Marginalised young people need specific opportunities to be listened to and become involved in their communities.

Discussion of the findings

Four main themes emerged from the focus groups:

Choice and responsibility

While many of their ideas for change require action by others, young people believe that principally it is up to them to change their own lives. Self-determination, choice and responsibility was a central theme to emerge from all the groups. Many young people said that when they were younger they had chosen not to listen to advice or warnings from parents and other adults. They had chosen not to go to school. They had chosen to join a particular peer group and to take drugs. They had chosen to start offending. A few were clear that they had decided to go on offending after release from prison. The majority said how much they regretted having made these choices.

From discussion in the groups, a more complex picture developed. There had been times when many young people felt seriously let down by adults who could have cared for them or helped them. Some had become marginalised and excluded from systems and institutions which seemed increasingly irrelevant. A number had conformed to what were seen as 'normal' patterns of offending behaviour in the places where they lived. But almost all the young people still held to the view that their offending was essentially 'down to them' and that they had some degree of choice about whether to get involved.

Once they had become caught up in an informal system of offending and in the formal criminal justice system many young people said that it was very hard to get out of again. Most saw not re-offending as primarily their responsibility. Their emphasis on personal responsibility would endorse the development of institutional cultures which stress pro-social behaviour and citizenship. Offending behaviour might be reduced by increasing opportunities for youth participation and involvement in the community and in secure settings. Peer support and victim reparation schemes would enable young people to take responsibility both for themselves and for others.

Parenting and families

In all the groups, the young people talked a lot about their families. Many spoke of disrupted lives: absent fathers, premature deaths and changing family relationships. One or two young women referred to abuse and neglect, although in general these issues were not introduced for group discussion. Some young people spoke of close support and guidance, particularly from their mothers. They discussed parenting from different perspectives: as children themselves; as carers of younger brothers or sisters; and as young parents. Most were trying to maintain links with family and close friends while in prison. Whether their experiences had been positive or negative, it was clear that almost all the young people ascribed considerable value to parenting and the role of the family.

Most young people did not want to see parents blamed for their children's involvement in crime. Yet, importantly when it came to discussing how they would parent their own children, many wanted to do things differently. They wanted to 'be there' for their own children, to communicate and 'get through' to them and to set clear, supportive boundaries for them.

The young people's emphasis on the importance of parenting would support a number of government initiatives which focus on the family including the Sure Start Initiative.

In regard to the crime reduction agenda, interventions designed to support, rather than blame, parents would seem to be more acceptable to the young people themselves. While none said that parents should be helped to parent teenagers, they did identify that communication between parents and teenagers needed to improve. This may be relevant to the application of Parenting Orders and the development of family support by youth offending teams.

The difficulty of resuming, or sometimes assuming, parenting roles and responsibilities was discussed by a number of young parents. Again, help was not sought directly but targeted support for young parents leaving custody might help them to be the good parents they say they want to be.

Professional adults and professional services

Above all, young people wanted to be treated with respect in a way appropriate to their age and developmental stage. They wanted to be taken seriously by professional adults. Many gave detailed practical examples of disrespectful treatment, clear abuse of power by adults in authority and, in some cases, incidents involving overt racism or violence. This has important implications for the selection, training and management of staff who work with vulnerable and volatile children and young people.

Almost all the young people said that they wanted the professional adults who care for them to be people who they can respect. They wanted staff who could relate well to young people but who would maintain professional boundaries. They wanted people who were reliable and straightforward. Constant personnel changes, particularly in probation and youth justice services were heavily criticised.

The young people identified unprofessional practices in the criminal justice system which included court bias and delays between arrest and sentencing, inaccurate report writing and failure to take account of reports. In prisons they were critical of failure to use induction, sentence planning and personal officer schemes and the way in which offending behaviour programmes, education and preparation for work schemes were often cancelled. Throughout the system, they wanted more consistency and transparency. They wanted clear rules and procedures suitable for people of their age. The Prison Service Order 'New Regimes for under 18 year olds' sets out to improve practice. One of the young people's principal criticisms of prison was that it neither connected with, nor prepared them for life outside in the community. The new Detention and Training Order aims to address this issue for under eighteen year olds.

Many of the young people's concerns about lack of professionalism are being tackled by the Government's agenda for reform of the youth justice system and the work of the Youth Justice Board. The impact of most of these reforms has yet to be experienced or evaluated.

Decent lives and decent futures

In each group, young people talked in detail about their everyday lives and what it took to survive. The young people defined what they regarded as decent lives and decent futures, with reference to their own, primarily negative, experiences and their hopes and fears for their own children. The key environmental features would be good quality housing and 'cleaned up' estates. There would be good opportunities for education and health care. Young people would have real jobs and be paid properly. Above all, there would be no drugs, no homelessness, no poverty and no crime. The Social Exclusion Unit have focused on a number of these same concerns.

Drug abuse, and to a lesser extent alcohol abuse, was discussed in all the groups. Addiction to hard drugs was seen as a primary factor in early involvement in crime and in re-offending. Despite their emphasis on self-determination and choice, most of the young people said they wanted help to stay off drugs. Drugs had become the thing to tackle, so much so that it was easy to miss the few references in the groups to why young people had started taking drugs. These were firstly their availability, including prevalence of use in the peer group and targeting of vulnerable young people by others. Secondly, drugs provided a temporary escape for many from what they described as 'shit lives out there'. Paradoxically, the drugs themselves had become almost impossible to escape. The young people's views would endorse the Government's commitment to tackle hard drugs at every level. Many believed that the difficulties of withdrawing from, and staying off drugs, are still underestimated.

The young people highlighted the need for complex solutions to complex problems. Their views support the Government's joined-up approach to tackling social inequalities as a way to reduce crime.

As far as almost all the young people were concerned, decent lives and decent futures did not involve crime. Crime reduction was very much on their agenda too. Many were critical of growing up in areas where crime and violence were just part of everyday life. Young people in this age group are more likely to be victims of crime than any other group. They did not want to be exposed to any more crime.

A primary concern in all the groups was both the fear, and the high probability, of re-offending. Most believed that it was up to the individual to stop offending but, in all the focus groups, the young people said that they needed considerable help from family, friends, prospective employers, and professional adults to do so. They also recognised that the Government had a vital role to play in bringing about change. They hoped that their voices would be heard, and their ideas taken seriously. As one young person said:

'Tell them so they listen'.

Appendix 1 Focus Group Outline Schedule

Family relationships & parenting

What was it like growing up in your family?
What was it like growing up in care?
Did your parents try to keep you out of trouble?
Are there adults who did try to help you out?
Were there things that adults did that made you stop and think?
What could the adults around you have done to stop you offending?
How easy is it to maintain links with your family whilst you are in prison?
Do you think it's useful for prisons like this to teach parenting?
Have any of you got children of your own?
Do you know whether there's a parenting course here?
    Would you go on it?

Education

How did you find being at school?
What age were you when you left?
Did you truant, why?
Did any of you get good things out of school?
Were there teachers that you got on well with?
Were there teachers that tried to help you out, stop you getting into trouble?
What could have made school a better experience for you?
Are any of you attending education courses?
How do you feel about education here?
Is it a different experience to being at school?
Are any of you planning to go back to education when you leave?

Offending and the criminal justice system

How would you explain how you got involved with offending?
Did drugs and alcohol have an influence?
Is there anything that would have stopped you following this route?
Before you got to prison, what were your experiences with the police?
What were your experiences with probation and social work?
What were your experiences with the courts?

Getting to & growing up in prison

How did you feel when you arrived here for the first time?
What do you remember about arriving here?
How did you feel during your induction and assessment?
How do the staff treat the young people here?
How could your relationships with staff be improved?
Where would you go if you had a problem and wanted someone to talk to?
Are their members of staff that you could talk to?
Do you have any contact with the prison governor?
    What is he/she like?
Do you talk to other prisoners?

Violence & bullying

Is bullying and violence common here?
What do staff do to prevent bullying?
What could be done to stop bullying here?
Is there anything that does lower the amount of bullying?
How do you deal with it if you know someone is being bullied?
Are there members of staff you could go to?
Did any of you experience bullying or violence when you were growing up?

Thinking about and preparing for release

In what ways does the prison help you prepare for life back in the community?
Are you being helped to look at job and housing opportunities?
Do you think you'll return to crime when you leave?
What could the prison do to help you prepare for life outside?

Note:
This outline schedule shows the topic areas which were covered in the focus groups. It gives examples of the kind of questions asked. The precise nature of the questions and the order in which the topics were explored varied from group to group.

Notes on TSA and the Authors

The Trust for the Study of Adolescence (TSA) was founded in 1989 to create an organisation which would promote the study of adolescence, and work towards a wider understanding of this stage of human development.

TSA produced the first specialist training to work with young men in custody[43] and the first gender specific training for staff in women's prisons[44]. Currently TSA is working with the Prison Service to develop a national accredited award based upon these programmes which aims to improve the quality and standards of work with young people in secure settings.

The youth justice programme at TSA includes management of the Cadbury Youth Justice Fellowship; an evaluation, funded by the Lankelly Foundation, of parenting training for young fathers in custody; and a partnership project with the University of North London which is exploring ways to increase resilience, and reduce vulnerability, amongst young women in care or custody.

TSA has a substantial programme of work focused on parenting support commissioned by the Home Office and the Youth Justice Board.

Juliet Lyon is Director of the Prison Reform Trust. Until January 2000 she was the Associate Director of TSA. She was responsible for professional development and consultation. In addition, she managed the youth justice and adolescent mental health applied research programmes.

Dr Catherine Dennison is Senior Research Officer at TSA. She has worked on a number of projects, including a three-year study of young people and communication. Currently she is evaluating the effectiveness of parenting training delivered in Young Offender Institutions and its sustainability after release.

Dr Anita Wilson is an independent prison ethnographer. She was employed by TSA to create accredited training for staff who work with young people in secure settings. She is currently a Research Fellow in the Centre for Research in Ethnicity and Gender at the University of North London.

---

43   The Nature of Adolescence: Working with young people in custody, Lyon & Coleman (1994, 1998).
44   Understanding and working with young women in custody, Lyon & Coleman (1996).

References

Audit Commission (1996) *Misspent Youth... Young people and Crime.* London: HMSO.

Boswell, G (1995) *Violent Victims: The Prevalence of Abuse and Loss in the Lives of Section 53 Offenders.* London: Prince's Trust.

Bright, J (1999) *Preventing Youth Crime.* In Francis, P and Fraser, P (Eds.) Building Safer Communities. London: Centre for Crime and Justice Studies.

Bullock, R, Little, M and Millham, S (1998) *Secure Treatment Outcomes. The Care Careers of Very Difficult Adolescents.* Ashgate: Dartington Social Research Series.

Caddle, D and Crisp, D (1997) *Imprisoned Women and Mothers.* Home Office Research Study 162. London: Home Office.

Catan, L, Dennison,C and Coleman, J (1996) *Getting Through: Effective Communication in the Teenage Years.* London: BT Forum.

Children's Express (1998) *Life on Estates.* Report to the Social Exclusion Unit.

Coleman, J (1999) *Key Data on Adolescence.* Brighton: Trust for the Study of Adolescence.

Crabbe, D (1997) *Psychological Effects of the Prison Environment.* Unpublished Conference Paper.

Davies, C, Archer, S, Hicks, L and Little, M (Eds.) (1998) *Caring for Children Away from Home. Messages from Research.* London: John Wiley and the Department of Health.

Emler, N and Reicher, S (1995) *Adolescence and Delinquency.* Oxford: Blackwell.

European Prison Educators (1998) *Report on the 6th EPEA International Conference of Prison Educators.* Budapest: Central and East European Information and Documentation Centre.

Farrington, D (1996) *Understanding and Preventing Youth Crime.* York: Joseph Rowntree Foundation.

Goldblatt, P and Lewis, C (1998) *Reducing Offending: An Assessment of Research Evidence on Ways of Dealing with Offending Behaviour.* Research Study 187. London: Home Office.

Graham, J and Bowling, B (1995) *Young People and Crime.* Research Study 145. London: Home Office.

Grindrod, M (1998) *Sentenced to Fail. Out of Sight, Out of Mind.* London: The Howard League.

Hayman, S (Ed.) (1996) *What Works with Young Prisoners?* London: ISTD.

Hayman, S (Ed.) (1998) *The Forgotten Children. Young People in Prison.* London: ISTD.

Hedderman, C and Gelsthorpe, L (1997) *Understanding the Sentencing of Women.* Research Study 170. London: Home Office.

HM Chief Inspector of Prisons (1997) *Young Prisoners: A Thematic Review.* London: HMSO.

HM Chief Inspector of Prisons (1997) *Women in Prison: A Thematic Review.* London: HMSO.

HM Chief Inspector of Prisons (1999) *Suicide is Everyone's Concern: A Thematic Review.* London: HMSO.

Hood, R (1992) *Race and Sentencing: A study in the Crown Court.* Oxford: Clarendon.

Liebling, A (1991) *Suicide and Self Injury amongst Young Offenders in Custody.* Unpublished Cambridge University Dissertation.

Lloyd, E (1995) *Prisoners' Children, Research, Policy and Practice.* London: Save The Children.

Lyon, J and Coleman, J (1994, 1998) *The Nature of Adolescence: Working with Young People in Custody.* Brighton: Trust for the Study of Adolescence.

Lyon, J and Coleman, J (1996) *Understanding and Working with Young Women in Custody.* Brighton: Trust for the Study of Adolescence.

Morgan, D (1996) Focus Groups. *Annual Review of Sociology*, 22, 129-152.

Parker, H, Measham, F and Aldridge, J (1995) *Drugs Futures: Changing Patterns of Drug Use amongst English Youth.* London: Institute for the Study of Drug Dependence.

Reiner, R (1992) *The Politics of the Police* (2nd ed.) New York: Harvester Wheatsheaf.

Rutter, M, Giller, H and Hagell, A (1998). *Antisocial Behaviour by Young People.* Cambridge: Cambridge University Press.

Utting, D, Bright, J and Henricson, C (1993) *Crime and the Family.* London: Family Studies Centre, NACRO and Crime Concern.

Utting, W (1997) *People Like Us.* London: Department of Health and the Welsh Office.

West, D (1982) *Delinquency: Its Roots, Careers and Prospects.* London: Heinemann.

Youth Justice Board (1999) *Speeding Up Youth Justice.* London: HMSO.

Publications

List of research publications

The most recent research reports published are listed below. A **full** list of publications is available on request from the Research, Development and Statistics Directorate, Information and Publications Group.

Home Office Research Studies (HORS)

191. **Domestic Violence: Findings from a new British Crime Survey self-completion questionnaire.** Catriona Mirrlees-Black. 1999.

192. **Explaining reconviction following a community sentence: the role of social factors.** Chris May. 1999.

193. **Domestic Violence Matters: an evaluation of a development project.** Liz Kelly. 1999.

194. **Increasing confidence in community sentences: the results of two demonstration projects.** Carol Hedderman, Tom Ellis and Darren Sugg. 1999.

195. **Trends in Crime Revisted.** Simon Field. 1999.

196. **A question of evidence? Investigating and prosecuting rape in the 1990s.** Jessica Harris and Sharon Grace. 1999.

197. **Drug Misuse Declared in 1998: results from the British Crime Survey.** Malcolm Ramsay and Sarah Partridge. 1999.

198. **Modelling and predicting property crime trends in England and Wales.** Sanjay Dhiri, Sam Brand, Richard Harries and Richard Price. 1999.

199. **The right of silence: the impact of the Criminal Justice and Public Order Act 1994.** Tom Bucke, Robert Street and David Brown. 2000.

200. **Attitudes to Crime and Criminal Justice: Findings from the 1998 British Crime Survey.** Joanna Mattinson and Catriona Mirrlees-Black. 2000.

Research Findings

83.   **Concern about crime: findings from the 1998 British Crime Survey.** Catriona Mirrlees-Black and Jonathan Allen. 1998.

84.   **Transfers from prison to hospital - the operation of section 48 of the Mental Health Act 1983.** Ronnie Mackay and David Machin. 1998.

85.   **Evolving crack cocaine careers.** Kevin Brain, Howard Parker and Tim Bottomley. 1998.

86.   **Domestic Violence: Findings from the BCS self-completion questionnaire.** 1999. Catriona Mirrlees-Black and Carole Byron. 1999.

87.   **Incentives and earned privileges for prisoners – an evaluation.** Alison Liebling, Grant Muir, Gerry Rose and Anthony Bottoms. 1999.

88.   **World Prison Population List.** Roy Walmsley. 1999.

89.   **Probation employment schemes in inner London and Surrey – an evaluation.** Chris Samo, Michael Hough, Claire Nee and Victoria Herrington. 1999.

90.   **Reconviction of offenders sentenced or released from prison in 1994.** Chris Kershaw. 1999.

91.   **Domestic violence matters: an evaluation of a development project.** Liz Kelly. 1999.

92.   **Increasing confidence in community sentences.** Carol Hedderman, Tom Ellis and Darren Sugg. 1999.

94.   **The Prison Population in 1998: a statistical review.** Philip White. 1999.

95.   **Using Mentors to Change Problem Behaviour in Primary School Children.** Ian St James Roberts and Clifford Samial Singh. 1999.

96.   **Meeting Need and Challenging Crime in Partnership with Schools.** Graham Vulliamy and Rosemary Webb. 1999.

97.   **The role of social factors in predicting reconviction for offenders on community penalties.** Chris May. 1999.

98.   **Community penalties for fine default and persistent petty offending.** Robin Elliott, Jennifer Airs and Stefan Webb. 1999.

99. **Demanding physical activity programmes for young offenders.** Peter Taylor, Iain Crow, Dominic Irvine and Geoff Nichols. 1999.

100. **The admissibility and sufficiency of evidence in child abuse prosecutions.** Gwynn Davis, Laura Hoyano, Caroline Keenan, Lee Maitland and Rod Morgan. 1999.

101. **Reconviction of offenders sentenced or released from prison in 1995.** Chris Kershaw, Joanne Goodman and Steve White. 1999.

102. **Jury excusal and deferral.** Jennifer Airs and Angela Shaw. 1999.

103. **The cost of Criminal Justice.** Richard Harries. 1999.

104. **Predicting reconvictions for sexual and violent offences using the revised offender group reconviction scale.** Ricky Taylor. 1999.

105. **Making the tag fit: further analysis from the first two years of the trials of curfew orders.** Ed Mortimer, Eulalia and Isabel Walter. 1999.

106. **Drug treatment and testing orders – interim evaluation.** Paul J Turnbull. 1999.

107. **The Victims Charter – an evaluation of pilot projects.** Carolyn Hoyle, Rod Morgan and Andrew Sanders. 1999.

108. **The Milton Keynes Youth Crime Reduction Project.** Alan Mackie and John Burrows. 1999.

109. **The nature and effectiveness of drugs throughcare for released prisoners.** John Burrows, Alan Clarke, Tonia Davison, Roger Tarling and Sarah Webb. 2000

110. **Home detention curfew – the first year of operation.** Kath Dodgson and Ed Mortimer. 2000.

111. **Attitudes to crime and Criminal Justice: Findings from the 1998 British Crime Survey.** Joanna Mattinson and Catriona Mirrlees-Black. 2000.

112. **Problem drug use and probation in London.** Ian Heamden and Alex Harocopos. 2000.

Occasional Papers

Restorative Justice: an overview. Tony Marshall. 1999.

Step 3: an evaluation of the prison sex offender treatment programme. Anthony Beech, Dawn Fisher and Richard Beckett. 1999.

The Impact of the National Lottery on the Horserace Betting Levy: Fourth Report. Sam Brand. 1999.

An assessment of the admissibility and sufficiency of evidence in child abuse prosecutions. Gwynn Davis, Laura Hoyano, Caroline Keenan, Lee Maitland and Rod Morgan. 1999.

Violence at work: findings from the British Crime Survey. Tracey Budd. 1999.

Demanding physical activity programmes for young offenders under probation supervision. Peter Taylor, Iain Crow, Dominic Irvine and Geoff Nichols. 1999.

Youth Justice Pilots Evaluation: Interim report on reparative work and youth offending teams. Jim Dignan. 2000.

New measures for fine defaulters, persistent petty offenders and others: the report of the Crime (Sentences) Act 1997 pilots. Robin Elliott and Jennifer Airs. 2000.

Requests for Publications

Home Office Research Studies, Research Findings and *Occasional Papers* can be requested from:

Research, Development and Statistics Directorate
Information and Publications Group
Room 201, Home Office
50 Queen Anne's Gate
London SW1H 9AT
Telephone: 020 7273 2084
Facsimile: 020 7222 0211
Internet: http://www.homeoffice.gov.uk/rds/index.htm
E-mail: rds.ho@gtnet.gov.uk